Protagoras
Nietzsche
Stirner

EXPOSITORS OF EGOISM

by

BENEDICT LACHMANN

translated by
EDWARD MORNIN

foreword by
KEVIN I. SLAUGHTER

appendix by
TREVOR BLAKE

UNDERWORLD AMUSEMENTS

Originally published in 1914 as
PROTAGORAS–NIETZSCHE–STIRNER:
EIN BEITRAG ZUR PHILOSOPHIE DES
INDIVIDUALISMUS UND EGOISMUS

Designed and edited by
KEVIN I. SLAUGHTER
with editorial notes by
SIDNEY E. PARKER

Translated by
DR. EDWARD MORNIN

Special thanks to
PÓL O'SULLIVAN, LEON PARKER, NATTY,
JEFF HARRISON, MARK A. SULLIVAN,
HUBERT KENNEDY & TREVOR BLAKE

Published by
UNDERWORLD AMUSEMENTS
ISBN: 978-1-943687-05-3
REV:XI.X.MMXIX

STAND ALONE
SA1090

More information at:
WWW.SIDPARKER.COM
WWW.UNIONOFEGOISTS.COM
WWW.UNDERWORLDAMUSEMENTS.COM

Foreword.

ALMOST LOST.

It was February of 2016 when I reached out to Hubert Kennedy, translator of *Max Stirner: His Life and Work*. I asked if he happened to have a copy of what appeared to be an obscure item I'd seen in passing. He responded that he wasn't aware of it.

This inquiry started just like many others in the course of my research to reveal the history of Egoism.[1] Find a reference to something I'm not aware of and follow it until a dead end. Pick it back up and find out more. Repeat until satisfied and move on.

In this instance I was at Johns Hopkins University library, using their microfiche reader to peruse some of the hidden treasures on Peace Plans microfiche I had just obtained.[2] I was skimming a copy of the New York Gay/Individualist Anarchist journal *The Storm!*, published by Mark A. Sullivan. There was a reference

---

1 UNIONOFEGOISTS.COM
2 LIBERTARIANMICROFICHE.COM

in a mid-80s issue to a forthcoming book containing original translations of two rare German works on Stirner. It was to be called *Two Essays on Egoism*, and contain both Benedict Lachmann's book *Protagoras, Nietzsche, Stirner: Ein Beitrag zur Philosophie des Individualismus und Egoismus* and *Max Stirners Philosophie des ich: ausgewählt und erklärt von Herbert Stourzh* (Max Stirner's Philosophy of The Ego, Selected and Explained by Herbert Stourzh).[3]

I began searching for a copy, for sale, at a library, a photo of one online, anything. The only reference I could find of it were in promotional materials published by The Mackay Society and an article by Sidney E. Parker from issue no. 7 of his journal *Ego*, published in 1986. That article, titled "The Egoism of Max Stirner" is a compilation of reviews of various English-language books about Max Stirner.

It was clear that this point that the book was never released. About a month later that I was able to uncover a second promotional blurb about *Two Essays on Egoism*, but this time it mentioned Dr. Edward Mornin was translating the Lachmann book. I'd seen Mornin's name associated with some of the work of the Mackay-Gesellschaft in Germany, and began searching for a way to contact him. I managed to reach him via email when he was on vacation. He assured me that he would look through his papers to

---

3   An excerpt from the still unpublished translation of Stouzh's essay was published in Sidney E. Parkers *Ego* Number 14 (1991).

try to locate a copy when he got home in a month. I was to find that not even Dr. Mornin retained a copy.

ನು

I finally made contact with Mark A. Sullivan, editor of *The Storm!* and The Mackay Society, near the end of 2016, but he didn't have a copy available either. If one *was* in his archives, he'd said, it was buried deep in storage, unlikely to be found for a while.

All seemed lost until another avenue broke open: the papers of Sidney E. Parker. It could be *proven* he had a copy *at one time*. In fact, besides Edward Mornin, he was the only person that I could prove had ever seen the manuscript.

By the time Sidney E. Parker died in 2012, he and his wife Pat had become reclusive, cutting themselves off from the world, including their family. So when Sid's son Leon emailed me one day in September of 2017 that he had 48 hours to clean out the old flat, before the Housing Council came in to *throw anything remaining into the garbage*, I had to act fast.

I contacted Pól O'Sullivan and Jeff Harrison. These two had been organizing meetings as the London Union of Egoists, and had both been in touch with Leon as well. They spent 8 hours sifting through decades of random papers hoarded into great piles in the small Notting Hill flat.

In an email to Leon, the next day, I wrote:

> Oh, before I forget, if you happen to run across a text titled *Protagoras Nietzsche Stirner* by Benedict Lachmann, translated into English by Dr. Edward Mornin,

that would be the only known copy in existence! Sidney reviewed it, but it was never officially published, and I was able to track down Dr. Mornin (who is in his 90s I believe!) and he can no longer find a copy in his own records!

Two days later, I get a brief but exciting response:

> "I've found it looking through piles of papers took out an envelope and it fell out."

Leon scanned the pages and emailed them in numerous batches. The story was not over though. For complicated reasons, a *second rescue* of Sid's papers was necessary. I went London this time, after a 72 hour notice. With help from my pal Ashley I rescued Sid's life's work and personal effects and papers, and shipped it to my home in Baltimore. There I established the Sidney E. Parker Archives.[4]

I am also very pleased that during the production of this book that Trevor Blake, my partner in the Union of Egoists project, acquired a complete run of Lachmann's journal *Der individualistische Anarchist*. Blake has translated Lachmann's "foreword," stating Lachmann's intent for the journal, and compiled an index of all twelve issues. These new works form an appendix at the end of this book.

KEVIN I. SLAUGHTER
November, 2018
Baltimore, MD

---

[4] WWW.SIDPARKER.COM

Protagoras. Nietzsche. Stirner.

I · Protagoras.

There are few philosophical problems as important for the general public as the problem of ethics. Whether the world as we perceive it really exists, and what its actual character is—we leave the solution of these and other metaphysical problems to the philosophers and the representatives of the various sciences. The place of the individual in the world as he himself sees it, however, and his relationship to the people around him and to the things confronting him each hour of each day—these questions occupy and interest each of us whether we like it or not. The place that each individual must occupy in the struggle for existence is generally determined by his place in society; custom, habit and tradition usually determine the weapons that we use in the struggles forced upon us. Since, in these struggles, the individual scarcely ever stands alone but, actively or passively, in relationship to others, conflicts and compromises arise in our dealings with others. The codification of the courtesy that a person demands or practises belongs to the realm of ethics, and it is our relationship to ethical laws, the laws of the society of which we are part, that interests most people most.

Thus we find that even in the earliest beginnings of philosophy, among the Greeks, it was the ethical problem to which most attention was paid. This, of course, is not a problem that can be solved independently of other philosophical problems, such as logic, metaphysics and especially the theory of cognition, and so we shall have to touch upon these other problems too.

Ionian natural philosophy, from whose appearance in the 6th Century B.C. the origin of philosophy is usually reckoned, had soon exhausted itself in its vain effort to explain the world of phenomena and interrelationships cosmocentrically. Whether they declared the basic substance from which the world of reality was created to be water (like Thales), boundless mass (like Anaximander), air (like Anaximenes) or some other substance—all their attempts were doomed to failure on account of the inadequacy of their scientific tools.

To be sure, Heraclitus of Ephesus brought new life into the rigid principle of one basic substance with his hypothesis of the perpetual flux of all things, but this too failed to contribute much to the solution of the basic question of all philosophy, i.e. the interrelationship of phenomena.

Parmenides was the first to introduce new viewpoints with his theory of the opposition between the unchanging essence and the deceptive appearance of things. This first created the possibility of bringing man as the subject (rather than object) of judgement into the sphere of philosophical speculation.

Though the ground, so to speak, had been prepared in this way by Heraclitus and Parmenides, the appearance of Protagoras was an event of momentous importance, decisive for the whole future development of philosophy.

With the sovereign power of genius, he shattered the timidly constructed theories and uncertain and tentative hypotheses, and in their place put that fundamental proposition which for millennia has been the basis for entire philosophical systems: "Man is the measure of all things, of real things that they are, of unreal that they are not. And as each thing appears to each man, so is it for him."

With admirable and genial daring, he elevated man to the centre of our worldview; more than that, he made him the subject of perception, not the object, and so left all the trodden paths behind.

Unfortunately, Protagoras's work "Truth," which opened with this proposition, has been lost, and for our knowledge of him and his philosophy we must rely on the meagerest reports. Yet even these are sufficient to give us some impression of his great and towering personality and to fill us with profound astonishment at how this genius looked clearly upon the world with a gaze far ahead of his time.

Benedict Lachmann

After the brief notices of Diogenes Laertius and Sextus Empiricus, we are in the main dependent upon Plato's dialogues "Theaetetus" and "Protagoras." These must be regarded with caution, however, since Plato certainly misunderstood a good deal of Protagoras and also reproduced much of his thought inaccurately in order to glorify himself or Socrates.

Protagoras, then, makes man the sole criterion of being, which distinguishes him from all preceding and contemporary philosophers. By "man" he means not man in a general or anthropological sense (as some people have maintained)—not all mankind, then—, but each individual. This clearly emerges from a passage in the "Theaetetus" dialogue.

Socrates asks: "Doesn't he (i.e. Protagoras) mean that each thing is for me how it appears to me, and for you how it appears to you?"

And Theaetetus answers: "That is what he means all right."

Let us now ask what Protagoras understood by the "measure of all things." Did the reality of phenomena exist for Protagoras? Was man as the "measure of things" only a judge of the properties impinging upon him from things? Did his "measure" correspond to actual being, beyond mere appearance? Or did man perhaps first create the phenomenal world by means of his imagination?

We find no answer to these questions in Protagoras. Yet we can answer for him from what we know: it is a matter of total indifference for man whether things beyond human judgement and conception also actually exist, since for all practical purposes the external world has only relative value for man. For Protagoras, it is unimportant whether things can be assigned a special reality over and above that. Not only individual sense perception was to be decisive, of course, but the sum of all knowledge obtainable by any possible means. Things possess significance and reality for a person in accordance with the extent to which he is willing and able to judge them. The theory of the constant flux of all things, when applied to the discernment of phenomena, leads to the relativity of all things. That is the basis of Protagoras's teachings.

These teachings inevitably caused hopeless confusion in the heads of Socrates' followers, who strove after a clear distinction between reality and appearance, and the few passages in the dialogues in which such contradictions are expressed are amusing and interesting.

Socrates-Plato, for example, even went so far as to remark: "I'm surprised only by the beginning of the proposition, by the fact that he doesn't begin his 'Truth' with the words: the measure of all things is the pig or the baboon or some other strange creature that possesses sense perception..."

How little Plato understood, or wished to understand, Protagoras's proposition!

Protagoras constantly stresses the necessity of extending our knowledge, and his whole manner of teaching and of training followers would be pointless in his sense if by man who is the "measure of all things" he understood only the individual contemplating the phenomenal world without any knowledge and trusting only in his sense perception. Even for such a person, of course, each thing is "as it appears to him." The world of a person possessing a limited horizon is just as limited as he is, but with knowledge one extends the possibility and ability of applying broader standards to the judgement of phenomena, of comprehending more of the world's things and so of applying a greater "measure." Relatively speaking, the phenomenal world is equally great for each individual, as great as he can grasp with the ability and knowledge that he possesses. Yet to conclude from this that it is futile to extend one's knowledge, totally contradicts Protagoras's teaching. For that reason, too, the best teacher is for him the wisest (i.e. the person who knows most). Briefly summarizing Protagoras's theory of cognition, we can say that for each person the phenomenal world is no more and no less than he himself can grasp. Just as things are in constant change and permanent flux, so too are man's knowledge and judgment of things. It is true that greater knowledge alters men's attitudes with regard to things, but this brings us no closer to answering the question of their absolute and qualitative existence.

Coming from Protagoras's radically individualistic theory of cognition, we must expect his ethics, too, to stand on the same foundation—namely that man, the "measure of things," is also the "measure of moral concepts." Yet our expectations are disappointed. Instead of subjectivism, we find normalism. Not the individual is the "measure" of ethical behaviour, but external constraint, which is laid upon him from outside his person.

In his ethics, Protagoras puts the "state" in the place of the individual. Its laws are to be authoritative, compulsory and absolutely binding for all.

If it appears that Protagoras is inconsistent here and untrue to his own ideas and his perception of the world, we shall soon see that the contradiction is only apparent. We must only look more closely at what Protagoras means by "state."

For him, "state" in only a concept, whose origins and purpose are exclusively practical in nature. The necessity of people living together created this association and its laws. The Greek Republics knew nothing of "divine ordinance" or suchlike terms with which we often enough are in the habit of ornamenting the concept "state" today. The "state" was nothing but a practical association and—in Protagoras's view—the absolutely necessary presupposition for the survival of the individual. It seemed as impossible to Protagoras as it still does to most people today that the individual could survive without a relatively strict association.

And because the "state" is necessary for the existence of the individual, the existence of the "state" is paramount.

We must bear these conditions in mind when

Protagoras asks: "Is there or is there not something in which all citizens must necessarily participate if a state is to survive?" And he gives the answer himself: "Most certainly there is."

Seen from this point of view, his normalism is transformed into an implicit subjectivism. Just as the individual is not an unchanging, unmoving mass, but is in constant flux, so too the "state" is always changing to serve the differing interests of individuals.

And now the relativism which declared man the measure of all things also breaks through, making the "state" the measure of ethical values.

With his characteristic boldness and clarity, Protagoras declares: "What each state considers just and beautiful shall be just and beautiful for it, until that state decrees otherwise."

Is there any greater relativism than this? Is there any sharper rejection of all strict ethical concepts than this clear, concise formulation?

Not only does "each" state determine what is just and beautiful, and so of course also what is unjust and ugly, good and bad etc., but it is bound to its decision only for as long as it is in its own interest to let it stand.

Consequently, all ethical concepts have only relative meaning for Protagoras, and we are astonished at the depth of his logic when he declares: "I call some (views) better than others, but by no means truer."

"Better" means here "of greater use to the state," to the practical association of "individuals." Protagoras rejects any other criterion for judging ethical concepts. In particular, he repudiates any supernatural justification of the sort advanced by the Oriental religions and, later, by Christianity by holding out the prospect of a reward after death for the "good" and of punishment for the "evil." He disallows such views for the simple reason that, as he himself said; "...we cannot know whether they (the gods) exist or not, for much prevents us from finding out—the obscurity of the matter and the brevity of human life." What a strong and powerful personality speaks to us even in these few words!

Again and again, in many other places, Protagoras emphasizes the relative value of all ethical concepts, and for him Plato's theory of ideas is as incomprehensible as Protagoras's teachings are for Plato. Practical as his philosophy is, it knows no "absolute good" or "absolute bad."

"However," he says, "I do know many things which nevertheless are *useful* to men (such as food, medicine and a thousand other things) and other things which are *disadvantageous* to them...and yet other things which are useless or advantageous to horses, but neither the one nor the other to men" etc.—

In accord with Protagoras's views on ethical principles is his opinion on the possibility of teaching virtue. Here, too, the principle of usefulness is the sole determinant.

"In my view justice and virtue are of mutual advantage to us, and so everyone should willingly teach his fellows what is just and lawful."

To develop man's capacity for justice is the concern of education. Parents, teachers and school, and above all life are successively and concurrently involved in the educational process. Later the state forces a man to become familiar with the laws and to act in accordance with them. All citizens in a state have a voice in deliberations concerning the welfare of the state. The wisest, however, he who knows most, exercises the strongest influence in shaping the law.

"Yet the wise man takes care that things that are good, instead of merely bad, for the state to come into being and achieve acceptance. And so some are wiser than others, though no one has totally false notions."

If it now seems that Protagoras's teachings are in danger of becoming entangled in the usual views on ethical concepts—for basically, of course, every state-association is a means of achieving the welfare of its citizens—we must once again recall the constant flux within the Protagorean state. For Protagoras and his idea of the state, there are no traditional or supernatural reservations, no positive concepts, but exclusively the practical standpoint of what is most useful. We must call his words to mind again: "What each state considers just and beautiful shall be just and beautiful for it, until that state decrees otherwise."

Yet he also says: "...far from denying that there is such a thing as wisdom and a wise man, I call that man wise who can turn us away from a belief in bad phenomena and badness to a belief in good phenomena and goodness."

"Good" and "bad," once again, are used here always in the sense of "useful" or "harmful" for the state, which is the necessary prerequisite for the existence of the individual.

❧

"Man is the measure of all things."

These words are written over the portal to individualism and egoism.

Behind that entrance the ways divide.

One way leads to the state as the necessary prerequisite for the existence of the individual. With the intention of developing a higher form of state and society and of mankind in general, it leads to the cultivation of separate individuals who direct the masses as leaders. At all times, however, the idea of the "state," "community" or "humanity" stands as a goal at the end of the way. This was the path taken by Protagoras and Friedrich Nietzsche.

The second way rises up more steeply and more boldly than the first. "As each thing appears to each man, so is it for him."

Via the dissolution of the "state" and of "humanity," it leads to the possibility of giving the individual the right to decide his own values, of making the individual's interests the centre of his own world and making him master over the things in it. This was the path taken by Max Stirner.

II · Nietzsche.

Protagoras's ideas on the relativity of all value judgments and on ethics as the theory of what is useful, never again disappear from the field of philosophy. Though pushed into the background from time to time, they nevertheless keep on appearing, at the varied periods and epochs, always having been developed further, always making use of new findings in the sciences. The same basic motif can always be heard: "Man is the measure of all things!"

Especially in ages of great ferment, those regularly recurring periods in which "the old" is overthrown to make way for "the new"—times in which everything is in a turmoil, changing its position voluntarily or under coercion—in such times this tendency usually acquires a stronger resonance. Whenever human society is at work coining new values, Protagoras's teachings become up to date.

In the course of the previous century, it was especially those great innovators Friedrich Nietzsche and Max Stirner who brought Protagorean relativism into the arena of public discussion, creating new friends and new enemies for it. Each time, this occurred in periods of great turbulence. Max Stirner's book *The Ego and His Own* appeared in 1844[5] that is, in the period immediately preceding the revolutions; Nietzsche's main work lies between 1874 and 1888, in the years when the labour question was just beginning to acquire its enormous importance in all civilized lands and when, in the intellectual sphere too, new names were at the focus of a not always objective criticism. Those were times, in short, when something "old" was once more to be replaced by something "new."

It might seem strange that I should give Nietzsche precedence in my investigations although he was still a baby when Max Stirner created his immortal work. I have considered this procedure more practical, however, for, as I see it, Nietzsche is further behind from the point of view of the development of the idea, and Stirner's teachings will in any event lead us further afield.

Among interested parties, it has long been a point of contention whether Nietzsche knew Stirner or not. The question has been answered in the affirmative with reasonable certainty, and without wish-

---

[5] Here Lachmann originally wrote 1845, which is the year printed on the title page of the Otto Wigand first edition, though it's generally accepted *Der Einzige* was actually released late 1844. We have made the same change in a later reference to this date, without further notation.

ing to dispute Nietzsche's originality; we will have to recall at certain points that Stirner was his predecessor and that Nietzsche, consciously or unconsciously, built upon Stirner, whom he did not name, just as much as he did upon Protagoras and many other philosophers whom he did name. Anyone involved with this topic must be struck by the great difference in popularity between these two writers. While Max Stirner was totally forgotten until John Henry Mackay brought him to the attention of the public again, and even today is still known to most people only by name, one finds Nietzsche's name on everyone's lips. And isolated catchphrases from Nietzsche's works are perhaps even better known than his name. It is quite unusual for laymen to be so familiar with a philosopher, and there must be reasons for this. First of all, of course, there is Nietzsche's brilliant and incomparable style; one might call him one of the outstanding stylists of the last century. Yet this alone would not be enough. It is my opinion Nietzsche acquired a considerable section of his admirers—who have not actually read him in his entirety, and indeed often not even in part—in the circles attracted by the markedly poetic character of his works and seduced by the mysticism and vagueness of his new teachings—a vagueness which suggests all or nothing at all. Over and above that, he certainly owed a great deal of the attention which he immediately attracted to the circumstance that his influence was felt most at a period when young people were for the first time demanding a hearing for themselves and for new values. Thus, many of the expressions coined by Nietzsche—I need mention only the catchword "superman"—were quickly accepted into the vocabulary of an age hungry for new values.

I have already mentioned the Mysticism and vagueness of Nietzsche's works. His teachings are—"as everyone knows," I may say—not recorded coherently or in clear and simple form, but are scattered throughout all his works, normally in aphorisms or parables, in short, in anything but strict scientific form. Nietzsche chose a poetic mode of expression, and this merits special notice. The poetic element in Nietzsche is extraordinarily strong, and if on the one hand this contributed to the rapid dissemination of his works, it also, on the other, led him into many an error.

There is no overlooking the fact that Nietzsche's works are full of contradictions; not only in works written at different periods, but in every single volume, we can find contrasting views and doctrines. I attribute this obvious lack of logic primarily to the predominance of poetry in Nietzsche. Instead of lengthy discussions, it is perhaps necessary only to let Nietzsche himself speak, from his letters, about his method of composition.

"Does anyone at the end of the nineteenth century have a clear notion of what poets of more vigorous eras called inspiration? You hear,—you do not seek; you take,—you do not ask who is the giver; a thought flashes into your mind like a bolt of lightening, inevitably, already shaped,—I never had a choice in the matter."

"Everything happens involuntarily to an extreme degree, but as if in a storm of passionate freedom, of absoluteness, of power, of godliness. The involuntary character of the image or the allegory is what is most remarkable; you no longer have any idea what an image or an allegory is; everything lies there before you as the most obvious and correct, as the simplest expression."

Sometimes Nietzsche describes how a word involuntarily sounds in his ear. Whoever knows poetic creativity knows how to value that divine inspiration which makes a poet—but not a philosopher.

As we read Nietzsche, we very frequently feel regret that his works cannot be evaluated purely as poetry, that he himself wished to be regarded as the founder of a new tendency in philosophy, and that his works as philosophy are in need of the closest scrutiny.

Their parabolic and aphoristic form also helped lead him astray into the realm of vagueness and, consequently, of contradiction, especially since the works were usually conceived and completed in an extraordinarily short time. It is all the more regrettable that Nietzsche, especially in his last years, lived all alone, without anyone possessing a sympathetic understanding of his works and yet with sufficient objectivity to draw his attention to what causes vagueness, misconceptions and contradictions.

What Nietzsche lacked in this respect during his lifetime has also been denied him since his death. His writings have been edited almost unabridged, which of course shows piety and is most valuable for any assessment of him as a poet, but certainly does not help his philosophical teachings any.

In his writings, as has been stated, Nietzsche does not develop along straightforward, consistent lines. Instead, we encounter frequent repetitions and alterations in his teachings, analogous to the above mentioned form and design of his writings. Nevertheless, there is no doubt that Nietzsche's development, despite all his deviations and detours, tends towards one specific goal, which we must keep in mind above all, if we are to judge his ideas.

That Nietzsche was quite outstandingly knowledgeable in Greek philosophy is too well known to require further special proof. It is just as well known that he studied the philosophers of the Platonic dialogues especially closely, and as an example of the influence of the Sophists on him it is enough to dispense with argument and quote Nietzsche himself: "Our modern way of thinking is profoundly influenced by Heraclitus, Democritus and Protagoras... it would suffice to say that it is Protagorean, for Protagoras assimilated both Heraclitus and Democritus."

We can feel the influence of Protagoras even in Nietzsche's last writings, and Protagoras's teachings provided the foundation stone for Nietzsche's own philosophy.

We are not interested here in Nietzsche's earliest writings, *Die Geburt der Tragödie* (*The Birth of Tragedy*), *Unzeitgemäße Betrachtungen* (*Thoughts out of Season*) etc. The germs of the later philosophy contained in these are scarcely worth mentioning. It was not until Nietzsche had liberated himself from Schopenhauer's influence that his later philosophical views began to manifest themselves in his grandly designed collection of aphorisms, *Menschliches—Allzumenschliches* (*Human—All Too Human*).

Strongly influenced by Darwin's theories, Nietzsche here constructs the matrix of his later works. He says, for example: "Men can now consciously determine to develop to a new level of culture, while formerly they developed unconsciously and randomly. They can now create better conditions for the emergence of man, for his nourishment, upbringing and education. They can administer the world as an economic whole and even balance men's strengths against each other or set them in opposition."

Human—All Too Human was written in the period immediately following Nietzsche's spiritual breach with Richard Wagner (1876). Certainly this event made the profoundest impression on him, and he experienced a most peculiar feeling, "that sovereign and sterile soaring above men, customs, laws and the conventional evaluation of things."

Nietzsche puts the "free spirit"[6] in the place of Protagoras's "wise man" and says of him: "...he became the counterpart of those who worry about things that do not concern them. In fact, the free spirit is concerned exclusively with things—and how many things!—that no longer worry him." Among the things that concern him is first and foremost an understanding of the world. This understanding is for Nietzsche, as for Protagoras, relative:

"Even if the existence of such a world (i.e. a metaphysical world) were convincingly proven, it would be certain that an understanding of it would be a matter of the most complete indifference."

Whether a world, then, actually exists or not outside of our perception of it, is unimportant for the individual living in it and passing judgement on it.

Especially the relativity of all moral views is frequently and emphatically stressed in this work and is illuminated from all sides.

Protagoras had taught that "good" and "bad," "beautiful" "ugly" are meaningful only with respect to their usefulness for the individual or the state (the extended individual) as the necessary condition for the existence of the individual, but that these concepts are anything but constant and absolute. We encounter the same train of thought at numerous points in Nietzsche's works: "We call that man good who, by nature, as a consequence of a long process

---

6   "A Book for Free Spirits" is the subtitle of *Human—All Too Human*.

of heredity, easily and willingly does what is customary, depending on what this is (e.g. who claims revenge when revenge is regarded as a good custom, as among the ancient Greeks). He is called good because he is good 'for something'; evil is to behave in an 'uncustomary' fashion, to act contrary to custom, to resist tradition, regardless of how reasonable or stupid it might be."

In another place, he says: "Regardless of all theology and everything written against theology, it is obvious that the world is neither good nor bad, let alone the best or worst of all possible worlds, and that these concepts 'good' and 'bad' have a meaning only with reference to people, and even here are perhaps unjustified in the manner that they are normally used. We must at all costs reject a world view in which the glorification of values or the vilification of those who deny those values plays a part."

The further question of who determines the value of "good" and "bad" is also answered by Nietzsche in the manner of Protagoras, who had said: "What seems good and useful to the state shall be good and useful to it until that state decrees otherwise."

Nietzsche says: "Morality is first and foremost a means of maintaining the community and preserving it from disintegration; after that, it is a means of keeping the community at a certain level and in a certain state of goodness."

We can also find numerous witty and shrewd formulations regarding the development of morality.

"Morality derives from two thoughts: 'the community is worth more than the individual'; and 'lasting advantage is preferable to temporary advantage.'"

At this beginning stage of morality, all individuality is suppressed for the good of the whole. The interests of the "community" exclusively determine "good" and "evil," and the community forces the individual to submit to it. Soon this restraint becomes "custom," then "voluntary obedience," and finally, through habit, the original constraint seems natural. The decision as to what is "good" and what is "bad" is still subject to the judgement of the "community," however.

Not even Nietzsche manages to navigate his way around this rock of contradiction.

On the one hand, all moral concepts are relative and in a constant flux; on the other hand, there is at first no possibility of the individual deciding for himself what is good and bad.

Protagoras and Nietzsche run aground on the notion that the welfare of the whole is more important than the welfare of each individual and that this can be achieved only through the establishment of moral concepts, any moral concepts, even though they are relative.

Protagoras got out of the fix by declaring that the wise man should be the leader.

Nietzsche does something similar. Firstly, he divides men into two caste: the powerful, and the powerless.

The morality of the powerful is different from that of the powerless. What seems evil or bad to the powerless is not so from the others' standpoint. "Each group has a wrong notion of the other."

Nietzsche explains the development of relationships between the two groups in accordance with the "principle of equilibrium": "In the beginning the community is the organization of the weak as a counterbalance to threatening forces." The weak form an association for protection against these forces whether they are natural forces or, in particular, "powerful individual wrongdoers." The desire to suppress the strong through a communal effort is actually very natural; yet this would lead to constant feuding, is extremely harmful to the general welfare. So the weak are content to arrange a defence that is an exact match for the influence of the powerful, that can counterbalance it. "Equilibrium is the basis of justice."

Yet this agreement, this equilibrium, is not a definitive condition, nor can or should it be.

"The legal *status quo* is, then, a temporary means, advised by prudence, and not an end in itself."

The struggle between the powerful and the powerless is constantly being renewed and continued. (Here again Darwin's influence is clearly discernible.)

Nietzsche combats in the most emphatic manner the solution that the socialists believe they have found: "If the permanent home of this welfare, the perfect state, were actually achieved, this welfare would destroy the humus from which great intellect and, altogether, the great individual grow: I mean strength and energy."

Nietzsche is also a zealous opponent of continual regard for the weak and of the organization of the state mainly for the protection of the powerless: "Christ—whom for once we shall regard as the most feeling heart in the universe—furthered the stupefaction of humanity, took the part of the poor in spirit, and hampered the procreation of the greatest intellect."

Thus, there is only one means of maintaining and improving the community, which for Nietzsche, as always, is the basis for the development of humanity: emphasis on the superiority of the powerful individual, of the strong-man. This is the point in which Nietzsche's philosophy culminates.

Even in *Thoughts Out of Season* Nietzsche says: "Mankind should constantly work on the task of bringing forth great individuals. This, and nothing else, is the duty of mankind."

At one point in his posthumous papers of 1874/77 Nietzsche expresses the same thought once more: "To bring forth great men the highest duty of mankind."

Nietzsche still vacillates between stressing the strong intellect or the strong will; he still denies freewill: "And so we reach the insight that the history of moral sentiments is the history of an error, of the error of accountability: and such it is based on the error of the freedom of the will."

"No-one is accountable for his actions. No-one for his being." Yet one can already catch a glimpse of the later doctrine laying strong emphasis on will, the doctrine of the will to power: "To make a whole person of oneself and to keep one's eye on the highest good of that person in all that one does—this advances humanity more than those sympathetic feelings and actions on behalf of others."

Here too, then, as in Protagoras.

To be sure, moral concepts are relative and unstable. The existence of the state, of the community, is the precondition for the existence and the welfare of the individual. Yet the "free spirit," like Protagoras's "wise man," achieves the "higher development" of the whole by becoming its leader and impressing the stamp of his powerful superiority upon it.

In *Morgenröte* (*Dawn*), which was written about three years later, and in the posthumous papers dating from the same period (1880/81), we find little more than mere repetition of the questions broached in *Human—All Too Human*. Here also the awareness of the relativity of moral concepts and values is repeated at too great length. Yet some points already sound more emphatic, more profound, more closely linked with later teachings.

Though the moral judgements which once possessed, and indeed still do possess, validity are assailed, and though their justification is opposed most energetically, the world must not be left totally without moral concepts.

Their very relativity makes them susceptible to change, and indeed creates the necessity of changing them in accordance with the dominant views of the age and, more important for Nietzsche, in accordance with the views of the future, the views that are to be striven after.

"Only if humanity had a universally accepted goal could one propose that 'we must act in this way or that'; in the meantime there is no such goal."

The relationship of the individual, especially the strong individual, to society, dominates a considerable part of the discussion. Searching arguments are advanced against socialism and its attempts at social levelling, and the emphasis on the strong individual, always of course as a means for the development of humanity, breaks through more and more. Again and again the motif is sounded: "Society has no goals other than great men and great works."

The question of power and rights, which Stirner answered in such an astonishingly clear and logical way, is also treated by Nietzsche here.

"Our duties—those are the rights of others over us. My rights—that is the part of my power that others have not only acknowledged but in which they are willing to support me."

The individual cannot, then, for example, decree and assert his rights from a standpoint of his own sovereignty, but "the others," "society," apportion "rights" to him.

The difference between the morality of the powerful and that of the powerless in *Human—All Too Human* is paralleled here by the difference between the working class—which includes anyone employed from early to late, including, then, "civil servants, merchants and soldiers"—and the "higher natures."

"In the long run this working class forces the higher natures to isolate themselves and form an aristocracy."

From this aristocracy the higher individual and the "community of free individuals" shall and will then develop.

It must be said here that this thought of a "community of the free" comes from Stirner, as we shall see again later. Quite characteristic for both thinkers is that while for Stirner it is merely the interest of the moment that determines the "community," Nietzsche immediately establishes and enumerates theses for his "free individuals." "They say," for example, "1. that there is no God, 2. that there is no reward or punishment for good and evil, 3. that good and evil derive validity only from the ideals and prejudices of the society in which we live," etc.

What has become of the "community of free individuals"? It has become a new society which once more sets up strict principles, new definitions of moral and ethical concepts.

Finally, in *Zarathustra*, we see breaking through and assuming clearer, more positive form the idea of the upward development of humanity and of the cultivation of individuals necessary for that.

The problem of cognition has vanished; all that matters now is the ethical problem, the relationship of man to man in an ethical context.

The path that Nietzsche appeared to be following for some time—saying that the higher development of the individual was the ultimate goal—is abandoned, and everything now appears from the viewpoint of the development of humanity.

The individual disappears as a phenomenon, as an isolated individual; now he exists only as part of a group, whether the group be "rabble" or "higher humanity." He exists only as a means to an end, to the goal of providing material for the development of humanity.

Nietzsche constructs the central idea of *Zarathustra*, the idea of the "superman," on two basic notions. The one is causal: the doctrine of the eternal return; the other is formal: the doctrine that "God is dead."

The idea of the "eternal return," already present in *Die fröhliche Wissensbhaft* (*The Joyous Science*), is a very important constituent part of Nietzsche's philosophy, yet it will be best to return to it in greater detail later.

The other idea—"that the old God is dead in whom everyone had once believed"—clears the way for the idea of higher development.

"But now this God died! You who are higher men

should know that this God was your greatest danger."

"It is only since He is lying in His grave that you have been resurrected again. It is only now that the great Noon will come; it is only now that the higher man will be—Lord!"

Inhibitions are overcome. The way is free for the higher man. Overcome is the preconception that anything in itself is "good" or "evil," that there is a *morality* for "strong" and "weak," that the world exists for the weak. It is acknowledged that "man is a bridge and not an end in himself."

Now the loud bell of the new gospel is rung out over the valley: "I shall teach you the superman. Man is something that must be overcome."

"Until now, all creatures have created something above themselves: do you wish to be the ebb of this great flood-tide and do you prefer to revert to the animal rather than to overcome the man?"

"What is great in man is that he is a bridge and not an end in himself. What can be loved in man is that he is a transition and a decline."

Man must go into decline, and a new being, the superman, must come into being, so that humanity, which has too long been slow in developing to a higher level, may progress.

Let us see how this central thought in Nietzsche's philosophy is developed further.

The next book, *Jenseits von Gut and Böse* (*Beyond Good and Evil*), does not actually keep the promise of its title. The relativity of the two concepts "good" and "evil" has already been repeated so often in the earlier works of Nietzsche's teachings. It is sufficient to say that the difference between "master morality" and "slave morality" is emphasized once again. One point speaks of "morality in the sense of a theory of hierarchical relationships under which the phenomenon that is life arises." Above all, however, we find a strengthening of the idea of the higher development of man. But it is no longer a matter of the development of "humanity," as was usually the case so far, but of the development of individuals, to whom in this book the word "aristocratic" (in contrast to the "common people") is frequently applied.

"Where the common people eat and drink, even where they venerate, it usually stinks."

The common people, society, are now no more than the basic level from which higher man should arise: "...so that society should not be there for its own sake, but only as a substructure and framework in which a select type of being may arise to fulfil its higher duties and, altogether, to achieve a higher form of existence."

"Every advance in the type 'man' has until now been the work of an aristocratic society."

New is the idea that it has always been the duty of the "many" to obey.

"The main thing 'in heaven and earth,' it appears, is—let me say it once more—long-term obedience to one will. In the long run, this produces and has always produced something for whose sake life has been worthwhile."

The appearance of "a leader who knows only how to command" (Napoleon) has a "beneficial" and "releasing" effect.

A few more words must be said about the "higher type," "the aristocratic type of man." This type "is aware of itself as a determiner of values; it decides that 'what is harmful for me is in itself harmful.'"

In *Zarathustra* we have already found a correspondence between the "whole" or "humanity" and the "higher man" or "superman."

"Humanity" is the basis on which and from which the "higher man" can and shall develop—this again only for the purpose of advancing humanity itself.

Nietzsche's next work—his last and most comprehensive—was *Der Wille zur Macht* (*The Will to Power*). Once more it embraces the main points of his philosophy, the doctrine of the "superman" and of the "eternal return." (*Götzendämmerung* [*Twilight of the Idols*] *Antichrist* etc. which were still to be written in the last year of his life, 1888, contribute nothing new to our topic.) These two themes are treated more positively here. Nietzsche is not satisfied with negative criticism, as he usually is in his earlier writings, but for his philosophy he sets up new ground-rules and principles according to which men should act and develop.

First of all, we find a critique of all existing values, partly as a repetition of earlier theories. If Nietzsche had previously asserted the relativity of moral values, he now goes beyond that. He speaks of "—moral values as a history of lies and of the art of slander in the service of a will to power (the will of the herd, which rebels against stronger men)."

All previously existing values can be understood only from the point of view of their having brought advantages to one group—and this group, according to Nietzsche, is the "herd." Henceforth, then, moral values are no more than weapons in the struggle between various groups of men.

"My proposition is this: that there are no moral phenomena, only moral interpretations of phenomena. These interpretations themselves originate outside of morality."

At another point we read: "...all these values, if we check them psychologically, are the results of specific perspectives of usefulness for the maintenance and strengthening of human hierarchical structures: they are only falsely projected upon the essence of things. It is still a sign of man's hyperbolic naivety that he sets himself up as the sense and standard of things."

This conclusion shows us how far Nietzsche in the meantime has—apparently—deviated from Protagoras's starting-point. I say "apparently," for as a standard of things he sets not some thing outside of "man," but the "higher man," the "superman"—that is, basically only "man."

And now we also discover what characterizes

the "higher man," the "superman": not one new or unusual characteristic peculiar only to him, nor the sum of suchlike characteristics. Rather he possesses all human characteristics developed to the highest degree: ruthlessness, inhibited by no anxious glances sidewards or back; full and powerful emphasis on his personality; strength to impress his stamp upon the world, the will to power;—those are the characteristics of the higher man!

"I teach acceptance of all that strengthens, all that stores up power, all that justifies the feeling of power."

"The affirmative passions:—pride, joy, health, sexuality, aggression and war, reverence, grace and beautiful manners, strong will, spiritual discipline, the will to power, gratitude to the earth and life—all that is rich and rewarding and all that enriches and glorifies and immortalizes and deifies life—all the power of *transfiguring* virtues, all that accepts, affirms and creates—."

The most important thing to emerge from the strong emphasis on all these passions, however, is the will to power. To *wish* to assert his personality is the supreme postulate for the superman.

"Whoever determines values and directs the will of millenia by directing the highest natures is the highest man."

"My theory is this: that the *will to power* is the basic form of passion, and that all other passions are merely manifestations of it."

If we now have an impression of the "higher

man," the "superman," the most important thing for us to know is how he stands with regard to humanity as a whole and how humanity stands with regard to him. First of all, humanity is still, as it always was, the foundation and matrix from which higher man should grow. Nietzsche also approaches this topic from a new angle, that of the theory of cognition. In so doing, he operates quite radically in negating everything and so clearing the way for a new theory of cognition suited to his own purposes.

It is his opinion, in short, that any theory of cognition is no more than an attempt to give power to the dominant group by interpreting perceived concepts in such a way as to affirm the values of that group.

"There is neither 'spirit,' nor reason, nor thought, nor consciousness, nor soul, nor will, nor truth: all of these are useless fictions. It is not a question of 'subject and object,' but of a specific species of animal which thrives only when its sense perceptions are accepted to be relatively *correct* and above all *consistent* (so that it can capitalize on experience)."

"Cognition works as a *tool* of power."

"The meaning of 'cognition': here, as with 'good' and 'beautiful,' the concept must be understood in a strictly and narrowly anthropocentric and biological sense."

"*The practical end of self-preservation*—not some abstract theoretical need not to be deceived—is the motive behind the development of the organs of cognition."

Yet Nietzsche's radicalism goes further still. He goes so far as to assert: "The properties of a thing are its effects on other 'things.'"

"If one thinks away other 'things,' then a thing has no properties, i.e. there is no thing without other things, i.e. there is no 'thing' in itself."

Here Nietzsche commits the grave error of simply making the human faculty of cognition and human thought the criterion of the absolute.

At any rate, the land is now cleared for new values.

"The categories 'purpose,' 'unity,' 'being' with which we have attached value to the world are withdrawn by us again—and now the world appears without values."

The way is now open for the higher man to stamp his values upon the world, unhampered by moral preconceptions. The absolute value of such judgements is unfounded, and their relative value is valid only with respect to the will to power.

It even appears that "Nature" demands the higher type of man, for Nietzsche says: "Morality is a countermovement to nature's efforts to bring forth a *higher type*."

Now the question arises: how does the "herd" conduct itself?

First of all, there should be a "hierarchy."

"Herd-sense should apply within the herd, —but should not extend beyond it: the leaders of the herd require a fundamentally different value system for their own actions; so do the independent spirits, or the 'beasts of prey' etc."

Yet society not only has the duty to provide material for the emergence of the higher man; it should also contribute what it can to making his appearance possible. This is achieved by means of purely practical, though sometimes very draconian, regulations. Granted: "It is a very recent idea and a very vague and arbitrary notion that humanity has a collective duty to absolve. Perhaps one will be rid of this before it becomes a 'fixed idea.'" Yet only a few pages later we read: "If an individual represents the ascent of the human race, then his value is indeed extraordinary; ...If he represents a decline, decadence, chronic sickness, then he possesses little value... In this case it is society's duty to *suppress egoism*."

It is part of society's duty to control conditions for the propagation of the race so that the higher type may develop.

"A medical record, preceding every marriage, and signed by the district magistrates."

"Every marriage sponsored and recommended by a certain number of trustees in the community."

"Society, as grand mandatory of life, is responsible for every failed life before the beginning of that life,—society must also suffer the consequences of such failures and so should prevent them. In many cases society should prevent *conception*..." etc.

It is Nietzsche's serious intention to cultivate

the superman. "Again and again we ask ourselves: ...given the increasing extent to which the 'herd'-type is being developed in Europe at present, is it not perhaps time to begin the fundamental artificial and conscious cultivation of the opposite type and of the opposite virtues?"

I mention this because, as will be indicated later, the idea of the "superman" has been presented by some interpreters as if it were not intended to be realized but was rather conceived of purely as an idea. For that reason, I want to indicate at this point already the absolute error of this view.

All that remains for us now is to deal with the idea of the "eternal return," to which Nietzsche has devoted a separate chapter in *The Will to Power* after touching on it repeatedly in earlier works. This idea was never expressed by Nietzsche himself in concise form: it can be grasped only by the subtlest means and actually leaves enormous latitude for arbitrary interpretation. We must first of all note that the idea constitutes one of the two basic notions in his philosophy, the other being the "superman." It can, then, be understood and explained only in connection with the idea of the "superman." The question arises: Is the idea of the eternal return the cause or the condition of the idea of the superman? or is it the necessary consequence of it? or are the two part of one comprehensive idea?—We find Nietzsche's first notes on the subject in a collection of aphorisms in his posthumous papers (1881) under the title of "the eternal return." He says here: "The amount of energy in the universe is specific, not *infinite*: we must avoid such excessive concepts! Consequently, the number of positions, changes, combinations and developments in this energy—enormously great and practically '*boundless*' though it may be—is definitely specific and not infinite. The time, however, in which the universe applies its energy is infinite, i.e. energy is infinitely uniform and infinitely active:—up to this present moment an eternity of time has already elapsed, i.e. every possible development must already *have existed. Consequently*, the development of each individual moment must be a repetition, as must also the moment that gave it birth and the moment that is born from it, and so on both forwards and backwards!..."

"Whether, *apart from that*, anything comparable has ever existed is totally undemonstrable."

Nietzsche, then, argues as follows: An eternal return implies firstly the energy (meaning of course the sum of all existing energies) *from* which repetition takes place, and secondly the time *in* which repetition takes place. Energy is not infinite but limited, though "immeasurable." Time, on the other hand—which Nietzsche, then, understands as an absolute concept in the sense firstly of being real and secondly of existing outside of and independently of "universal energy"—*is* infinite. Now Nietzsche continues that "every possible development must already have existed," for—"an eternity of time has already elapsed." Here is the grave error that overthrows his theory. What is the meaning of: "an eternity of time has already elapsed"?! Is there more than one eternity?! Surely not! And yet the characteristic of "eternal" time is precisely that it never "elapses," neither "forwards" nor "backwards." We shall argue the contrary: namely that if an infinity of time is necessary for a repetition, no repetition can have occurred or ever can occur, for infinity is never reached since that would contradict the concept "infinite."

It is an open question whether a repetition is possible, i.e. conceivable, *within a part* of "infinite time." Nietzsche never asked this question or dealt with this hypothesis.

If we assume, with Nietzsche, that time is "infinite" in contrast to energy, which is limited, then there might be the *possibility* of a repetition within a part of "infinite time."

Yet even then we do not arrive at any concrete or even conceivable result. Let us call the sum of all existing energies X. Since all energies are mobile and must be taken into consideration, the sum of all possible manifestations of energy is X^X, a notion which we can neither imagine nor apply to any practical end.

Let us not forget, incidentally, that the number X expresses all energies and combinations of energies existing in the *universe*, and not only those which happen to exist on this little earth of ours.

I said that we cannot apply the result that we have reached to any practical end, because we cannot imagine it. That is what matters in this case, for Nietzsche uses the idea of the eternal return to lend impetus to his doctrine of the superman.

There are also some other attempts at metaphysics demanding our attention. Among them are a few hypotheses which we must reject very emphatically—for example, when Nietzsche says:

"Space, like matter, is subjective form; *time* is not. Space first came into being through the assumption of *empty space*. There is no such thing. All is power."

I question each one of these lapidary statements!

Nietzsche also employs analogies—the most dangerous form of "proof"!

"An affirmation arises from two negations if the negations are energies (darkness from light against light, coldness from heat against heat etc.)."

Let us now turn to the question that interests us most. Granted there were in fact an eternal return, what does it mean for Nietzsche and his idea of the "superman"?

Psychologically, it is easy to understand how Nietzsche—the conscious and proud creator of new values, of quite shockingly new values indeed—should wish these values to last for eternity and not merely for a short period. It is in this light that we first see the idea of the eternal return as a basis for the "superman." If we are convinced of the eternal return, it is obvious that man will return on a progressively higher level of development.

Indeed, even if the eternal return were an illusion, an error, belief in it would have enormous importance as a spur for the higher development of humanity.

"Idea and belief lend a weight that presses down upon you together with all other weights, and more heavily than they."

"If you assimilate the idea of ideas it will transform you. In all that you do, the *greatest* weight is brought to bear by the question: 'Is this the kind of thing that I want to do countless times?'"

"Let us examine what has been the effect thus far of the *thought* that *something* is *repeated* (the year, for example, or recurrent epidemics, waking and sleeping etc.). Even if circular repetition is only a probability or possibility, the very *thought of a possibility* (not only feelings or specific expectations) can shake us and transform us! How enormous has been the effect of the *possibility* of eternal damnation."

Nietzsche more or less substitutes his doctrine of the eternal return for the religious concepts of heaven and hell.

"Let us impress the image of eternity on our own lives! This thought contains more than all the religions that despised this life as transitory and taught men to look towards another, indefinite life beyond."

These views of the year 1881 are repeated in the same or similar form in the later collection *The Eternal Return* (1888).

One addition is the application (to the idea of the eternal return) of Nietzsche's new "theory of cognition," which he had developed in the interim. Just as all values are meaningless except as a means of strengthening the power of the ruling class, so can the idea of the eternal return, as a factor lending value, become a selecting principle for the higher development of man.

The question as to the relationship between Nietzsche's two main ideas can, then, be answered more or less as follows: The idea of the eternal return is a basis on which the idea of the superman is constructed, a foundation lending this idea resonance.

I have another question, however. The eternal return—originally it was even called "the eternal return of the same"—*insinuates* that everything has already existed before. My question is: *Does this include the superman*? For if he *had never yet existed*, this would be absolute proof against his *possibility*!!

If we now bring Nietzsche's teachings together as a whole, without being distracted by the deviations of individual periods and by their manifold contradictions, we form the picture of an aristocratic individualism.

Humanity has the goal of developing to ever-higher levels. The means to this end is not the slow and gradual advance of the totality, but the emergence of individuals, of strong characters, of leaders who by the power of their personalities will set their stamp upon the world in which they live. Moral concepts have only relative value and should hold only for *those* classes for whom they are suitable: a herd-morality for the herd and a separate morality for the "higher men." The idea of the eternal return acts as a stimulus for the planned development.

What position does this aristocratic individualism occupy among the other philosophies? The antithetical relationship of the individual to the totality expresses itself in two basic ideas:

1. The totality is more important than the individual.
2. The individual is more important than the totality.

To the first group belong altruism (Christianity) with its doctrine of "One for All," and socialism with its doctrine of "All for All." To the second group belong individualism with its doctrine of "All for One," and egoism, which breaks the concept "totality" up into "individuals" only and knows only self-interest.

Though the groups overlap to some extent, this contrast nevertheless helps to clarify the opposition between them. Altruism, socialism and individualism—unlike egoism—resemble each other in that they demand moral values and attempt to establish a specific purpose for the development of humanity. They also proceed from the standpoint that no event in the body social occurs fatalistically but that every event serves a notion of development, each philosophy regarding its own central principle, elevated to the status of an ideal, as the culmination of this development. Every doctrine that pursues a specific goal needs ideals, guidelines and goals. Regardless of whether these are understood as relative or absolute, they are totally indispensable. Egoism, unique in this central point, knows no moral concepts of any sort, neither relative nor absolute; it knows only subjective value judgements.

Nietzsche's aristocratic individualism has ideals, and he requires the establishment of values even though they are declared relative; he, i.e. his philosophy, cannot dispense with values entirely.

It is in this point that we find the closest links between Nietzsche and Protagoras.

Like Protagoras, Nietzsche teaches the relativity of moral concepts. Protagoras is unwilling to dispense totally with moral judgements. So too Nietzsche. Protagoras teaches that the community, the state, declares that to be good and useful which is good and useful for it; Nietzsche teaches that moral judgements are to be understood only as necessary for the convenience and self-preservation of the community that has established them.

There is a difference and a contrast here. Protagoras establishes this link between state and morality as a postulate: "that is how it is to be." Nietzsche verifies the fact—but criticizes it. He does not say: "that is how it is to be"; instead this problem is at the centre of his critique.

It is assumed as given that every social group determines its moral values in accordance with its self-interest. Three questions then arise. Why is this so? Is it desirable to change this state of affairs? If so, from what standpoint and in what direction?

The first question can be answered roughly as: for reasons of self-preservation. One would be digging one's own grave to defend anything other than what is "good" and "useful" for one's own purposes.

We can answer the second question in the affirmative, from the Nietzschean standpoint, only if, like him, we regard mankind's having a purpose as a given fact—to be more precise, having the purpose of developing to a "higher level." Without in the meantime investigating what this "higher level" consists of, the necessity arises of altering moral values in such a way as to realize the development of mankind in the desired direction. That also answers the third question.

If we ask what is mankind's ultimate purpose, we cannot give a precise answer. The creation of the "higher man" is actually not the final goal of the development, but the *means*. Yet it is the nearest goal, and the only one presented to us.

It is impossible to reach this goal by means of a peaceful understanding. Today's values form the basis for the existence of today's social order; they are the most precise crystallization of the compromises reached by the various involved power groups in order to achieve their own survival, and their surrender would inevitably be linked with the destruction of present-day society.

A society willing, then, to accept values other than those created by it would necessarily—and against its wishes—have to adjust to this altered standpoint; for, logically, it would be impossible for it to do so voluntarily, since voluntary acceptance would imply that it was recognized as necessary, which at the same time would bring about the desired social order.

Consequently, it would be necessary to attempt the desired "re-evaluation of all values" by means of conflict. If in this an enormous majority were pitted against an insignificant minority, this would prove nothing as to the outcome of the struggle, which would of course largely be fought with spiritual weapons.

Are these weapons strong enough? *For now the main question arises*: Why should we believe that "humanity" *has any goal at all*, and *why*, if there is a goal, *should it be the goal of the "superman" and nothing else*?

The individual and also humanity are parts of "universal energy," for nothing organic or inorganic exists without universal energy. The development of humanity is, then, irrevocably subject to the laws to which the energies themselves are subject—which, logic apart, all our experience confirms (birth, growth, death etc.). If Nietzsche, then, does not want his "re-evaluation" to be understood as wholly arbitrary—in which case he could just as logically require the opposite—he must indicate or at least assume reasons which *naturally* (i.e. in accordance with the laws of natural development) demand *this* development *and no other*. We can reject as absurd any notion that nature has *consciously* set humanity a goal. The logical necessity of *this* development and no other would have to derive, then, from binding reasons. Pointing to the evidence of history, Nietzsche expresses the view that humanity always took its greatest steps forward through the intervention of great personalities. Apart from the fact that one can differ in opinion as to what are the "greatest steps forward" and the "great personalities" and their relationship to each other, we must reject this argument alone on the grounds that the consequence of these influences from great personalities—reactions too are no more than necessary consequences—is precisely the present-day situation. We must demand that arguments conforming to the nature of things be produced for the necessity of the required "re-evaluation" outside of present-day and former values and social forms. These must be altogether eliminated, for not only positive, but also negative values are preconditions for the present constellation of social forms. Through the emphasis on or rejection of these, then, no "re-evaluation" can be undertaken in keeping with nature.

To justify the re-evaluation of values, new relevant reasons must be produced lying *totally outside of present or former conditions*. No such reasons can be produced from the realm of human capabilities and characteristics. Nor did Nietzsche produce such ideas, for he named only the idea of the "eternal return" as a further justification.

I have actually already produced my objections to this idea: If there is any such thing as an eternal return, and it can only be a return of the *same* (for otherwise it is not a return at all), there must already have been an infinite number of returns, and so also of the desired "re-evaluations" and "supermen," and in the eternal succession we would always have reached the shadow side in the certain consciousness that natural development in its eternal return will carry us to the sunny side again.

There is no way out of this labyrinth of confused wishes and facts through the medium of obligatory re-evaluation, and we must realize that we cannot force this re-evaluation against natural and inexorable development.

In an awareness of the contradictions in Nietzsche's philosophy and of the fact that the two main ideas "superman" and "eternal return" cannot be reconciled with scientific laws, the attempt has been made to interpret these ideas as if Nietzsche had not believed in their realization, as if he had wanted merely to hold them up to humanity as an ideal and as a stimulus. Such interpreters would have us believe that the "superman" is a constant challenge to man, growing with him, and that the idea of the "eternal return" is a constant reminder to man that: "You must live as if you were to return eternally."

I must firmly reject the suggestion that this was Nietzsche's view. The opposite is clearly evident through references (see above) in specific texts by Nietzsche.

Nietzsche has never proved that the "welfare of humanity," humanity's further development, depends on the emergence of the "higher man," the "superman." We can find no justification for this in natural development, and so it remains the philosopher's *personal opinion* that it is the goal of humanity to bring forth the "higher man."

What is the goal of humanity? What is the "higher man"?

Who can answer these questions? Is the goal of humanity Christianity, atheism, Buddhism?

Ask a Christian, a Jew, a Buddhist! Ask a negro, a worker, a scholar, a priest, a scientist! And see what they answer!

Who is the "higher man"?—the Christian, the Jew or the atheist?

Ask them all and ask anyone who will listen—and hear what they answer!

Where is the critic who can go beyond his own judgement and interest to make decisive judgements and issue decisive directives?!

The "higher man," the "superman," is as much or as little a higher man as any other type. He is just one of the manifestations that the human spirit can *imagine* and has as much or as little value as any idol that wishes to *force* a way and a goal upon human development.

The *question of questions* is: Is it possible to approach the solution of the social question with preconceived ideas? Is there any one key at all to open the door and let light shine in upon the mystery shrouding human relationships? Is there a goal for the development of mankind of the sort assumed by individualism as well as by altruism and socialism?

This is the *answer of answers*: all the thoughts and acts of the individual and of the totality have *one* foundation: *self interest*! This is valid for valuation and re-evaluation: if there is an interest and it is strong enough to assert itself, then it will do so. If not, it is dissipated and is worthless from the stand point of development.

The struggle of conflicting interests: that is the question of questions, and with that we have reached the "egoist" and Max Stirner.

III · STIRNER.

I have already indicated that Max Stirner was forgotten until John Henry Mackay rescued him and his works from oblivion and tried to win for him the place becoming his great and towering personality. The history of Stirner's re-discovery, his biography and the fundamentals of his ideas are recorded in Mackay's *Max Stirner: sein Leben und sein Werk* (Max Stirner: His Life and His Work) (Berlin, 1910), and when we read this interesting book a picture of the most radical of egoists takes shape before our eyes. Mackay deserves such special credit because there was no contemporary biography of Stirner (or anything resembling it). Furthermore, all of Stirner's friends are dead now, and the sole surviving person to have known him personally, Baroness v.d. Goltz, whom I succeeded in tracking down some years ago, could tell me nothing new.

Of all Stirner's writings, we are interested mainly in his greatest work *Der Einzige und sein Eigentum*

(*The Ego and His Own*), in which he has recorded his ideas, or, to be more accurate, has set down his understanding of the world. His other writings also contain in part germs of the same views, but since everything that he has to tell us is contained in his main work, we can and will restrict ourselves to it here.

It is not possible within the narrow framework of this work to reproduce Stirner's overwhelming personality in its entirety as we encounter it in his writings, and I must limit myself, as with Nietzsche, to stressing specific passages in his book in order through them to trace the development of his ideas. In contrast to Nietzsche's work, Stirner's is written in a clear, precise form and language, though it avoids the pitfalls of a dry, academic style. Its sharpness, clarity and passion make the book truly shattering and overwhelming. It appeared in 1844, strongly excited public opinion at first and provoked a flood of the most contradictory criticism, and then was completely forgotten in the years of the Revolution. It goes deeply into the relationships between men and resolves into their basic elements the complicated circumstances in men's lives and the connections between them. Then, proceeding from the results of this investigation, it draws the astonishing conclusions of Stirnerian egoism. From what the history of the individual and of humanity teaches and reveals to him, he draws his logical conclusions, uninfluenced by any preconceptions.

Like Protagoras with his proposition "Man is

the measure of all things," Stirner too jumps into the midst of complex systems with the opening words of his book: "I have founded My cause on nothing."

Actually the short opening chapter already contains Stirner's entire credo *in nuce*, and he exposes a world of prejudice to our eyes when he says: "What isn't supposed to be My cause! Above all the Good cause, then God's cause, the cause of humanity, of truth, of freedom, of mankind, of justice; then the cause of My people, My prince, My fatherland; finally even the cause of the spirit and a thousand other causes. Only *My own* cause should never be My cause."

"What about humanity, whose cause We are to make Our own? Is its cause someone else's perhaps and does humanity serve a higher cause? No, humanity looks only to itself and seeks only to benefit itself. Humanity is its own cause."

"I do not need to demonstrate that everyone who would like to thrust his cause upon Us is concerned only for himself and not for Us, only for his own welfare and not for Ours. Just look at the others. Do truth, freedom, humanity and justice desire anything other than that You should become enthused and serve them?"

"And won't You learn from these shining examples that it is the egoist who has the best of the bargain? I for My part will learn from this and, instead of serving those great egoists further, will Myself be the egoist."

"God and humanity have founded their cause on

nothing, on nothing other than themselves. Let Me, then, likewise found My cause on Myself, who, as much as God, am nothing to all others, yet am My all and am unique."

"Away, then, with any cause that is not wholly My own cause! You say that My cause must at least be the 'Good Cause'? Enough of Your good and Your bad! I Myself am My own cause, and I am neither good nor bad. Neither word has any meaning for Me."

"The Divine is God's cause, and the cause of Humanity is 'man's.' My cause is neither the Divine nor the Humane; it is not the True, the Good, the Right, the Free etc., but it is exclusively *My cause*; and it is no universal cause, but is—*unique*, as I am unique. Nothing matters more to Me than Myself!"

We can follow Stirner in his essentials in the design of his book, whose first part is entitled "Man" and whose second part is entitled "I." Though Stirner does not always adhere strictly to this division, the design and execution of the work is a masterpiece of logic and clarity, and the enjoyment of reading it is incomparable. Stirner's first purpose is to describe man in relationship to his surroundings and to expose the reciprocal relationship between man and his surroundings. So, with a few characteristic strokes, he sketches the life of a man and, parallel to it, the life of humanity by juxtaposing the stages in a man's life with the stages in the development of humanity. The development considered by Stirner extends only as far as the middle of the last century, of course, and so some of the topical dogmas that he opposes seem to us antiquated and obsolete.

Nevertheless, this does not invalidate his criticism as a whole, for—give or take a little technology and "enlightenment"—the "spirit of the development" has remained the same to this day. Thus a considerable part of his criticism, particularly in the first part of the book, is directed at the most recent attempts in that period to assign "man" a new place in the world, and Stirner makes this criticism the foundation for his own ideas. It is especially Bruno Bauer and Feuerbach at whom Stirner directs his criticism.

"Man is the highest being for man," says Feuerbach.

"Man has only just been discovered," says Bruno Bauer.

"Let us, then, look more closely at this highest being and this new discovery."

The way in which Stirner investigates "concepts" is fundamentally different from any previous method. Any criticism concerned with a concept, no matter how relative it takes that concept to be, is basically directed at its interpretation, its evaluation, its context and suchlike. The concepts themselves, however, remain. Criticism of the concept "morality," for example, is directed at its interpretation, for some say "to be moral is to be religious," while others say "to be moral is to be charitable." Criticism is never directed at the concept "morality" itself, however, and no-one would dare to question the absolute necessity of morality.

Stirner describes the life of an individual. From the moment of its birth, the child is in conflict with all things around it; it confronts them as a realist, trying to find its way among them and to "get behind things"; consequently it spies out "all their weaknesses" and feels secure once it has got behind them; it has overcome them. In order to overcome them, it needs "cunning, intelligence, courage and defiance," i.e. "spirit."

"Spirit is the first form of self-discovery."

Unlike the child, the *youth* does not try to get behind things, but to get behind the "spirit of things." He is an idealist. He encounters forms of resistance different from those that the child had encountered.

"If in childhood one had to overcome the resistance of the *laws of the universe*, one now encounters in all one's undertakings the objections of the spirit, of reason, of *one's own conscience*." Unlike the child's thoughts, the youth's are not directed at the thing itself, but at the meaning of the thing. The child, of course, had been able to think too, but it thought only about the thing.

"We thought, then, that this world that We can see was made by God; but We did not think about (investigate) 'the depths of the Godhead' itself."

The youth tries to "bring *pure thought* into the light of day." Spirit is acknowledged as what is most essential, and striving is directed towards the fulfilment of the spirit, for in the meantime one has only ideals, i.e. "unrealized ideas or thoughts."

"The *man* differs from the youth in that be takes the world as it is instead of finding it deficient in every regard and wishing to improve it, i.e. to model it after his ideal; in the man, the view is established that one must deal with the world according to one's *self-interest*, not according to one's ideals."

So the man discovers himself as "embodied spirit."

Stirner finds a parallel to this brief overview of an individual's life in the history of mankind. He talks of the "men of ancient and of modern times."

The "ancients" lived in the feeling that the world as they perceived it was the real and actual world, and that actual relationships were incontrovertibly real and true. So, like the child, they confronted things as realists, but, like the child again, they tried to "get behind things." In the process, they encountered the enormous resistance of nature. "How little man can master! He must let the sun follow its course, the sea transmit its waves, the mountains jut up into the sky. He stands powerless before the invincible." Against these powers, there is only one weapon—"spirit"! Whether the ancients used it like the Sophists or the Stoics, they used it to free themselves from their oppressive feeling of impotence. They formed things after their spirit, their reason, and overcame their terror. Once on their way, they did not restrict themselves to the phenomena in their immediate vicinity; other relationships too, such as the natural relationships between human beings, were regulated by "spirit," which, however, as in the child, had not yet thought about thoughts.

As the Sophists operated with reason, so did the Sceptics operate with the heart. If Socrates had taught that it was not enough to make whatever use one pleased of reason and that one must use it in the "good cause," "the investigation of the heart had begun," and the attitude of the Sceptics was the final, logical consequence of this. It is only now that man is indifferent towards the existence or non-existence of the world. He has found his place in it by overcoming it "with his spirit." Consequently, his spirit is progressively sharpened through observation of the perceptual world, and perception becomes "acuteness." So the "moderns," the "Christians," inherited a world whose reality was overcome by spirit. Now, like the youth, they strive to get behind the spirit.

That is spirit? "It is the creator of a spiritual world." Yet it is "real spirit only in a world proper to it."

"It is in the nature of the matter that spirit, which is supposed to exist as pure spirit, must be ethereal, for since I am not spirit, it can only be outside of Me. Since a human being is not wholly absorbed in the concept 'spirit,' pure spirit, spirit as such, can only be outside of men, only beyond the world of men. It cannot be earthly, but must be heavenly."

So the spirit which was to overcome the world created a new world for itself, and soon we see everything populated by "spiritual beings."

"Out of the sweet little flower speaks the spirit of

the creator who made the flower so wonderfully; the stars proclaim the spirit that created order among them; from the mountain tops a spirit of sublimity blows down to Us; from the waters a spirit of longing rises like a sigh; and—a million spirits speak out of men. Though the mountains sink, the flowers wilt, the vaults of heaven collapse, and humanity perish—what does the destruction of these visible bodies matter? Spirit, 'invisible' spirit, is everlasting!"

This is how the double world comes into being: the real world in which we live, and the spiritual world which survives our bodies and which consequently is the "Absolute." The "Absolute" is "Truth" itself, and the truth is "sacred."

We are now only one short step from that spiritualization of what remains, of the whole world, that Christianity has realized. Just as "spirit" created a new world for everything, so now it creates new "concepts" for its new world. Not "men of flesh and blood" matter, but the concept "man." Human properties, like the individual himself, are only external manifestations of the "real truth." If "spiritual" man, not the "man of flesh and blood," is the "real man," how could "mankind" be the "real man"?

Beyond this understanding of what constitutes true humanity, validity is attributed to changless, true, and consequently "sacred concepts": "Sacred are truth, justice, law, the good cause, the monarchy, marriage, the common good, order, the fatherland etc. etc."

All of these and a thousand other concepts are

immune from man's judgement and criticism, for behind their outward appearance lies their true, spiritual, immutable essence.

This confusion of concepts is deeply rooted in us—so deeply that not even the free-thinker can truly liberate himself from them. A person is of course free to reject many "spiritual concepts," but he will put others in their place. He will perhaps deny God without denying the "concept of the Godhead." He can have a different understanding from other people of "honour" for example, but will he deny the "concept of honour" on that account?

We are all deeply enmeshed in this chaos of "concepts" and "essences" which are held up in front of our lives like distorting mirrors.

Stirner calls these "spiritual concepts" "beams" or "fixed ideas."

He says: "What do You call a 'fixed idea'? An idea which has subordinated man to it."

"Is, for example, the tenet of faith that must not be doubted, the sovereignty (of the people, for example) that must not be assailed, the virtue that the censor must allow no word to offend so that morality may be kept pure etc.—are these not 'fixed ideas'?"

"Whoever doubts them—attacks the *Sacred!* Yes, indeed, a 'fixed idea' is truly sacred!"

Feuerbach had established a new thesis: he put "man" in the place of God, and God's commandments became humanity's commandments.

"But only the god is changed," says Stirner. "The

Deus, love, remains; there love for the superhuman God, here love for the human God, for the *homo* as *Deus*. That is to say that man for Me is—sacred. And all that is 'truly human' is for Me—sacred!"

"Marriage is in itself sacred," says Feuerbach, "and so it is with all moral relationships. Friendship, property, marriage, the welfare of all men are and should be *sacred* to you. Yet these things are sacred *in and for themselves*."

No matter how one turns, the "sacred," the "true," what is independent of the individual, remains and is not destroyed, is not eliminated. It is only replaced by a new "sacred thing." Feuerbach has deposed God all right—but he puts a new God, "man," in His place, and a new religion arises.

The world of "fixed ideas" assaults the whole man. It engenders self-denial. Whoever is addicted to a fixed idea denies himself and his own desires "before God and the divine law." Selflessness! This means working for a goal which is of no advantage to the person doing the work. It means devoting one's life to a "sacred idea" like a "benefactor of humanity" or a "fanatic," like St. Boniface or Robespierre or Theodor Körner.

"*Fixed ideas* give rise to crimes. The sacredness of marriage is a fixed idea. From this sacredness it follows that infidelity is a *crime*."

"Fixed ideas also express themselves as 'axioms, principles, standpoints' etc. Archimedes required a standpoint *outside* the earth in order to be able to move it. Men continued to search for this standpoint unremittingly, and everyone assumed the stand point to the best of his ability. This external standpoint is the *world of the spirit*, of ideas, thoughts, concepts, essences etc.; it is *Heaven*. Heaven is the 'standpoint' from which the earth is moved and from which our earthly endeavours are surveyed and—despised."

Stirner has characterized the relationship of the "spiritual world" to our everyday world most aptly by means of this comparison. Behind and above every thought and feeling stands a regulating "sacred truth," "the real idea," the "absolute idea."

"In the presence of the sacred one loses all one's sense of power, all one's courage: one's relationship to it is one of impotence and humility."

All "virtues" such as "humility, submissiveness, servility" etc. have their origins here. An entire hierarchy, a "dominion of the spirit," comes into being.

"One circumstance which tangibly influenced the course of history after the birth of Christ was the effort to make the sacred spirit *more human*, to bring it closer to men and men closer to it. Through this, it could in the end be understood as the 'spirit of humanity' and appeared more appealing and familiar and approachable under various expressions such as 'idea of humanity, mankind, humaneness, universal love of man' etc."

Before we pursue this development further, let us now ask how the "world of the spirits" gained such control over man and so subjected him as to make him a caricature of his true self.

Primitive peoples know of no "world of the spirit." They confront their gods man to man, and a regular commerce controls the relationship between them: I sacrifice to you and worship you; you protect me and kill my enemies.

He saw how the "world of the spirit" found its firmest support in Christianity. Should we, then, look upon it as a specifically Christian achievement? I cannot affirm this unreservedly, for I see "fixed ideas" preceding Christianity too. Indeed, even when we think of Protagoras's proposition about "What each state considers good and beautiful" etc., do we not already find in the concept "state" the germ of a "spiritual concept"? And can we not see how even enlightened free-thinkers to whom Christianity and its teachings mean nothing are attached to "ideas" and cannot get away from them? Think of Feuerbach himself and Bruno Bauer, those two sharp critics of Christianity. Stirner also gives us a few pointers for the exploration of this phenomenon.

"Here We encounter the age-old delusion of the world which has not yet learned to dispense with priests. This delusion states that it is man's calling to live and work for an idea and that his *human* worth should be measured by how truly he has fulfilled that calling."

"How does it come about in the meantime that the egoism of those who maintain self-interest and consistently ask where this interest lies, nevertheless succumb again and again to a priestly or schoolmasterly (i.e. an ideal) interest? The reason is that their person seems to them (and indeed is) too small and insignificant to be able to claim everything and assert itself fully. A sure sign of this is that they divide themselves into two persons, an eternal and a temporal, and at all times care only for the one or the other, on Sunday for the eternal, on workdays for the temporal, in their prayers for the former, in their work for the latter. They have the priest within themselves, and that is why they are never rid of him and why they hear themselves receive a dressing down inwardly as if it were Sunday."

This second passage gives us some indication, of course, why it is that even free-thinkers and people who are particularly intent upon their self-interest cannot free themselves from the idea of the "world of the spirit." No more than the first passage, however, does it give us a complete and exhaustive explanation of how the "world of the spirit" could gain such strong and, above all, lasting influence. How did the world come by the "primitive delusion" that it was man's calling to live and work for an idea?

Stirner does not give us an explicit answer—but his book is his answer. In its final consequences, it offers the solution to the problem of the prime and deepest cause of the phenomenon. I see the cause in man's belief that co-existence is possible only on the basis of strictly ordered associations (family, nation, state etc.), and I see the phenomenon originating from the earliest beginnings of human intercourse, from the exchange of goods. To make a living, our primitive ancestors had to resort to exchanging goods, and given the dissimilarity of these goods they had to rely on a method which even today—though in the most complex form—underlies our trade and social intercourse, namely credit. These two factors together, interdependence and credit, form the basis of the virtues which are still valued today, e.g. honesty and suchlike. Out of self-interest, everyone, no matter what he thought personally, was obliged to honour generally recognized conditions if he did not want to lose his sole means of existence, namely the chance to exchange goods. In this way, there first gradually developed strict concepts concerning moral values. Later these concepts acquired "spiritual essence," making them immune from any individual judgement. Many people perhaps had their own views on the concept "honesty"; yet they still submitted to the "higher concept" in order not to damage their own interests. Here too we see the reason why in our age *moral* "fixed ideas" are much more enduring than *religious* ones, for example. The Heaven of religion has already lost much ground, and there are already many people attempting to dispense with fixed ideas in the religious sphere. Observe, on the other hand, the "Heaven of moral values." Loyalty, veracity, honesty, decency etc.—these concepts stand immovably firm as higher essences of the "world of the spirit," and no matter how they are interpreted from time to time, in accordance with changing taste, the "Sacred" itself must not be assailed. The more realistic the age—the more realistic the Heaven of the "world of the spirit." Are we still unwilling to learn from that how much the latter is a reflection—a distorted reflection—of the former? Do we still refuse to acknowledge how, even in the earliest beginnings, in the creation of the "world of the spirit," self-interest was the prime and moving factor?

Once man had begun to coin universally valid judgements and values, he soon extended this practice to other areas by way of God and other agencies, and the development of humanity, as we have traced it with Stirner's help, encouraged the creation and development of "fixed ideas." Just imagine what an influence on all virtues the concept of a "vengeful God," for instance, must have had. —Once "universally applicable values have been found, once the "world of the spirit" has been created, parents take care that these concepts live on in their children.

"There is a great difference," says Stirner, "between feelings and thoughts *stimulated* in Me by experience and those *given* to Me. God, immortality, freedom, humanity etc. are impressed upon Us from childhood as thoughts and feelings."

"Who has never noticed, consciously or unconsciously, that the purpose of Our entire education is to engender *feelings* in Us, i.e. to inspire them in Us artificially, instead of leaving the creation of them up to Us regardless of the form they might take. If We hear the name of God, We are supposed to feel awe; if We hear the name of His Royal Highness, it is to be received with reverence, veneration and servility."

"Stuffed full of *artificially inspired feelings* like this, We appear at the bar of adulthood and are 'declared to be of age.' Our equipment for life consists of 'ennobling feelings, sublime thoughts, inspiring axioms, eternal principles' etc."

If, then, we wish to answer the question as to how the "spirits" and "fixed ideas" gained such control over us, we must say: It is because men live in strictly ordered associations. Until such times as they unite exclusively for their own interests, whatever these may be, "fixed ideas" will not vanish from the earth.—

Let us now pursue this development further. Stirner devotes a major chapter of his book to the "free men," whese representatives he divides into three categories: the political, the social, and the humane liberals. Stirner shows us how even radical revolutionaries, even the most radical, have their "fixed ideas." The French Revolution made a clean sweep of kings and of the rule of the privileged classes—but only to put "the nation" in their place.

"This new *sovereignty* was a thousand times stricter, more severe and more stringent. Against the new sovereign there were no more rights or privileges; how limited in contrast is the 'absolute sovereign' of the *ancien régime*."

"With the era of the middle class begins the era

of liberalism. Its goal is 'reasonable order,' 'moral conduct,' 'limited freedom,' not anarchy, lawlessness, selfhood."

A whole new series of "higher beings," of "spiritual beings," of "saints," has come into existence. The old gods are dead; the new gods reign.

"In the citizen-state there are only 'free men' who are *forced* to do thousands of things (e.g. to show reverence, to have a religion etc.)."

The dominance of "fixed ideas" becomes even stronger under the aegis of "social liberalism," from which in our time socialism and communism have developed. The main idea is now "society." It is lacking in substance, is a concept, an abstraction, a "spirit." But it is a wicked tyrant! Under political liberalism "people had become equal," for there was only one remaining class, the "citizen class." Under social liberalism "property too is to become equal." "Henceforth let no one possess anything; let everyone—go begging. Property is supposed to be *impersonal*, to belong to—*society*."

"The opinion is voiced again that society *gives* what We need and that consequently We are *in duty bound* to it, that We owe it everything. People insist on wanting to *serve* a 'highest giver of all that is good.' That society is in no sense an individual that could give, award or grant, but an instrument or *means from which We may derive benefit*; that We have no social duties, but merely Our own *self-interest*, in whose pursuit society must serve Us; that We owe society no sacrifice, and that if We sacrifice it should be to Ourselves—the socialists never think of these things because, as liberals, they are ensnared in religious principle and zealously striving after a *sacred society* (of the sort that the state previously was)! The society from which We receive everything is a new taskmistress, a new spectre, a new 'highest being' 'inducting Us into service and duty'!"

To cap it all, the "humane liberals," that group of moral philosophers and suchlike public benefactors, are striving after the total "dominion of ideas." It is no longer enough that everyone *must* work in order to live (which is what socialism wants); now not only the work itself, but the very goal of this work should be "universal," not "private."

"Work must further mankind, aim for the welfare of humanity, serve historical (i.e. human) development. In short, work must be *humane*."

"The individual has no right to an opinion, but as individual will was transferred to the state and property to society, so must individual opinion be transferred to a universal concept, 'man,' thus becoming universal human opinion."

"Man" and "humanity" are two mighty "spirits," the supreme idea (varying only according to time and place) of the properties that would fill men if—they were not simply creatures of flesh and blood. We can trace the development of fixed ideas down to the present day and we will always encounter that constant succession of old gods being deposed to have new gods put in their places. In all spheres, excepting the sphere of the pure sciences, where number and logic mean everything and vagueness means absolutely nothing, we find the "world of the spirit" and "higher beings" in countless numbers.

If we see "humanity" as a whole pursuing everlasting phantoms in this fashion, we need scarcely inquire further about the attitude humanity adopts towards the individual. Any exception granted the individual would inevitably overturn the whole edifice. It is not enough for those so desiring to run after "fixed ideals"—God forbid!—, but everyone must pay homage to the generally acknowledged principles. The first principle is that "society" and "the people" are entities "higher than" the individual. So too are "family" and "state."

The actual relationship between "state" and individual is "that the state has no regard for My person; that I, like everyone else, am only one human being without any further significance that might impress the state."

"Citizenship is no more than the thought that the state, all in all, is the 'true man,' and that the individual's human value resides in being a citizen."

"The state is supposed to be a community of free and equal individuals, and everyone is supposed to devote himself to the 'welfare of the whole,' to be absorbed in the *state*, to make the state his goal and his ideal."

As does the state in a political context, so also

does "human society" demand absolute recognition for its "fixed ideas" in moral concerns. Dare to deny the necessity of a generally applicable morality, of ethics and so forth, and you will be expelled from an environment which, of course, you did not choose, but on which you depend for your living. You may go your own way in trivial matters and, depending on your taste, will be called eccentric or vivacious. But do not shake the foundations of the "eternal, universal principles," the "idea of humanity"!!

Whoever attempts to negate these "universal principles" and in all his doings pursues his own interests alone, is an "egoist." "*My own* cause should never be My cause."

Let us now refer back to Stirner's introductory passage: "What isn't supposed to be My cause! Above all the Good Cause, then God's cause, the cause of humanity, of truth, of freedom, of mankind, of justice; then the cause of My people, My prince, My fatherland; finally even the cause of the spirit and a thousand other causes!"

That indeed is how it is! A thousand other causes which I have not chosen as my own cause, a thousand "spirits," a thousand "fixed ideas" and concepts that I am supposed to make my cause!—Yet—Stirner asks further: "What about humanity, whose cause We are to make Our own? Is its cause someone else's perhaps, and does humanity serve a higher cause?. No, humanity seeks only to benefit its own cause."

Should we accuse Stirner of a contradiction

here? We saw, after all, that "humanity" has made an "ideal" of "higher entities," that it has made "ideals" of "morality," "charity," "ethics" and a thousand other "higher entities." That is true—but "humanity" does not serve these, but rather has made them its cause! Its own cause, not God's cause, or any other extraneous cause! Heaven forbid! *It has made these its own cause*!

And—let us pursue the reasons for this! Why has humanity made these "higher entities" its cause? Why can it not free itself from them? Why does it continue to let one new "fixed idea" arise from the ashes of the other? Why does it demand everyone's respect and will not tolerate egoism, special interests, the exclusivity of the individual?—Because the existence of the above-mentioned "concepts" and of all the gods proclaimed "higher beings" by humanity is necessary for humanity's existence—is the first and most important precondition for its existence. Just as humanity itself is not of this world but of the "spirit world," it cannot, as an "idea," exist from the properties of living men, of men of flesh and blood. It would disintegrate into the millions of actual individuals. For that reason, humanity, itself a "spirit" must derive the elements for its existence from the "spirit world." Self-preservation and egoism are the reasons why "humanity" demands our service in "its cause."

As it is with "humanity," so is it also with the "state," the "people," the "family" and all those others who require our service for their egoistic goal of self-preservation.

"The state requires that I do nothing that might endanger its permanence; *its permanence*, then, is supposed to be sacred to Me. I am not supposed to be an egoist, but an 'honest, upright' (i.e. moral) man. The main thing is that I should be totally compliant and respectful to it and its permanence and so forth."—

Do not object that we ourselves, the totality of individuals, are the "state," the "people," the "family"! These are "concepts" which force their dominion upon us and attempt to make us believe that archaic superstition according to which humanity is necessary for the existence of the individual!

Are "humanity" and the "state" also subject to all those laws which we are bound to obey as "sacred commandments"? Certainly—if they are *in the interest of "humanity" and the "state"*! Otherwise—all at once a "higher being" appears—the "higher interest" takes precedence (i.e. the interest necessary for the survival of "humanity" or the "state"). Is murder not forbidden everywhere at all times, and is it not prosecuted by humanity and the state?—Without a doubt that is so! Yet ask history how many thousands have been murdered in wars—for *interests of state*! But wars, you see, are waged for "honour" or some "just cause" or other!—which of course does not prevent the opponent from *losing* in a "just cause."

As it is with murder, so too is it with oath taking.

"If," says Stirner, "I had sworn to a person under investigation that I would not testify against him, the court would demand my testimony despite the oath binding me and, if I refused, would imprison me until I had decided—to break my oath."

And is lying not permitted in the *interests of state* or of some other "sacred community"?—despite the fact that the commandment states: Thou shalt not lie! Stirner gives us the example of a spy who falls into the hands of the enemy and is in duty bound to spread false information. However, there are in fact countless occasions on which "sacred commandments" must be violated—in the interests of the state or of other "higher entities."

"The end justifies the means!" This means that "immoral means" are permitted if they are "justified" by the "end"! What isn't "justified" these days!!

The "state," "humanity," the "Church" etc. are at least honest enough to admit that they are concerned about their egoistic cause, their self-preservation. Just as they know only egoistic interests, so too does an individual's every act basically derive from egoistic motives, and the very obligation to suppress these in favour of "general interests, higher interests" brings about an unnatural and indeed degrading ambiguity. This creates what Stirner aptly calls the "reluctant egoist": "the man who is always intent upon his own interests and yet does not consider himself the highest being; who serves only himself and at the same time always believes he is serving a higher being; who knows of nothing higher than himself and yet enthuses about higher things, in short about the egoist who would like not to be an egoist and debases himself; who coats his egoism, though at the same time debasing himself only 'in order to be exalted,' that is, in order to satisfy his egoism. Because he would like to cease being an egoist, he looks around in Heaven and earth for higher beings to serve and sacrifice himself to; but no matter how much he may exert himself and castigate himself, in the end he does everything for his own sake, and the egoism which he decries will not leave him. That is why I call him the reluctant egoist."

Society of course will—and in its own interests must—not suffer egoism. Society demands that men in all their actions should consider society's interests and respect and protect society's "concepts." It cannot tolerate the sovereignty of the individual because this would eliminate society. For that reason, in your actions you are supposed to bear in mind "human qualities," "social demands." In your neighbour, you should see only an image of mankind, and if you love the individual, you are not to forget to take into account whether that individual is a creature with "human qualities" fulfilling the requirements of "society." Dare to love a whore, who sells herself to everyone!——

Yet let us pursue further the egoistic motives for human actions. Why does the pious man live in accordance with the commandments of the Church and religion? "So that he may prosper in Heaven and on earth!"—Is this not egoism?—And yet, someone objects, there are certainly actions which cause the individual discomfort, effort and sacrifice and which benefit the "community at large" and are, then, not egoistic—such as charity, selflessness, bravery in war etc. But is there not concealed behind these actions, as behind all others, a person's need to express *his* feelings, *his* will, *his* temperament, and to satisfy *his* wishes? Would anyone, voluntarily, move into the first line of fire if he did not need to distinguish himself or to fulfil *his own* love of his fatherland? That these actions benefit others too, and also "society at large," is a side effect and not the deeper reason for the actions. These "reluctant egoists"—egoists who are egoists without knowing it or wanting it—also believe of course that they are inspired for a "good cause," for a "higher idea"!

"Just know Yourselves!" Stirner exclaims. "Just acknowledge what You really are and abandon Your hypocritical striving, Your foolish mania to be something other than what You are."

The more deeply one looks into the history of humanity and of each individual, the more clearly one perceives that egoism, the need to fulfil *one's own* will, is the driving force behind every action. What we must remember is that "state," "society" and "humanity" do not wish us to serve *our own* interests, but to make *their* cause (the cause of the state, of society, of humanity etc.) our cause—Yet, someone objects, do they not allow the individual sufficient freedom?

Do we not have intellectual freedom, freedom of thought, press, religion and many other freedoms?! Let us look more closely at these our much vaunted freedoms! First of all, let it be noted that what another gives me, namely all these freedoms, are gifts and so not my natural possessions. Relations between the individual and the "universals" (whether they be called "state," "people," "religion," "family") are regulated by laws in which rights and freedoms as well as prohibitions are expressed. We have already seen that all laws are in the interest only of the "society" that created them, and "rights" and "freedoms" too are only such as either benefit society at large or at least do not harm it. Every contravention of the law is punished, and the individual is obliged to submit to this punishment. Of what nature, then, are these rights? The individual has the right to life, property, work; he has civil rights, family rights, the legal right to school and other public institutions etc. Does this mean anything more than that, since he submits to the sovereignty of the society in question, he is making socially permitted use of institutions established for the benefit of *that same society*? May he permit himself a right that society has not sanctioned? Certainly not? Well now—with what "right" can "society" defend its interests within the law? By means of force!: The rights of society extend to the limits of the force that it can exercise!: An individual's right is what he *may* do, not what he wishes to do! Not what he himself wishes as "his right," but only what society through its powers decrees to be "his right"—that is his right!

"Whoever has power has rights; if You have no power, You have no rights."

"Society of course wishes everyone to have his rights, but only the rights sanctioned by society, only social rights, not *his own* rights."

"The criminal, then, gets his rights when he suffers what he risks—for why did he risk it when he knew the possible consequences? Yet the punishment that We mete out to him is only Our right, not his right. Our right reacts against his, and he 'is in the wrong' because—We get the better of him."

Can anyone seriously believe that the state or any society would grant an individual a right that ran counter to its interests?! Since it has the power—insofar of course as it has the power—all individual rights are only an expression of what the society in question allows him by virtue of its power, just as it forbids him other things by virtue of that same power. (One should recall the extraordinary similarity of Nietzsche's definition at this point.) It is also unavoidable that the various "societies" (state and Church, state and family etc.) should come into conflict among themselves over the distribution of rights. Every family has rights over its members. Yet let it try to keep the husband at home by means of its legal claims when the state calls him to arms! The "right of the state" is "higher," for—its power is greater than the family's!—Every citizen has the "right" to practise his religion.

For Jews, Saturday is a holy day. Yet the state demands service from Jews on this day too; it curtails their "religious rights"—for its power is greater. When the Church was stronger than it is now, Emperor Heinrich had to go to Canossa—in this conflict the Church was "right." Yet some years ago the French state made short work of the clergy; it was "the state's right" to act in this way—for it had the power to do so!—Every page in the history books and every day in our present lives show us the same picture. The "rights" of individuals and of any group are only as great as their power. Whatever the individual can achieve in any way—is his right! Someone objects that the criminal who steals and keeps what he has stolen because he is not caught does not possess it "by right." Well—as long as he possesses it, he possesses it by *his* right, not by society's right. *Society's* "right" forbids him to posses these stolen goods, but he makes use of *his own* "right"—as long as he has the power, as long as he is not caught!

"Right in itself," "higher right"—is a "fixed idea," a "spiritual entity" like a thousand others!

As it is with "rights," so is it too with "freedoms." The freedoms given us by society are granted insofar as they, like "rights," are in its interest, and society takes good care that they are not infringed or exceeded. We have freedom of thought and of speech. Yet just dare to express aloud a free thought which runs counter to the interests of the state! We have freedom of religion! Yet just dare to voice your opinion on religious matters insofar as they endanger the interests of the state! The state passes a law against duelling: "Two men who agree that they are willing to commit their lives to a cause (whatever the cause may be) should not be permitted to do so. The state does not wish it, and sets a punishment upon it. Where is freedom of self-determination here?"

There are few concepts with which so many vague demands are associated as the concept of "freedom." Everyone wants some freedom or other, and everyone possesses some or several freedoms.

Varying like the demands for various freedoms is how they are granted by those who control these freedoms—an alternation between demand and fulfilment. Strong pressure engenders the longing for liberation. Soon those who feel the longing are strong enough to liberate themselves from the pressure, and freedom "reigns." It *reigns*! For now it presses upon the previous oppressors, and the game begins anew! Yet it is always a "society" that grants the freedom—whatever particular freedom serves society's own interests; Are we supposed to believe, some people exclaim, that everyone should have "complete freedom"? ——What does "freedom" actually mean? Let us take freedom of the press for example.

"There are certain confusions surrounding the call for freedom of the press. What people ostensibly demand is that the state should *make* the press free; what people actually want, however without really knowing it; is that the press should be free of or rid of the state. The former is a *petition* to the state: the latter is a *revolt against* the state. As a 'petition for rights,' even as an earnest demand for the right of freedom of the press, it presupposes the state as a giver, and one can only hope for a gift, Permission, a decree from above. It is of course possible that a state may be so absurd as to grant this gift once it has been demanded; but You can be certain that these who receive the gift will not know how to make use of it as long as they regard the state as an Absolute: they will not transgress against this 'sacred entity' and will call for a punitive press law against anyone daring to do so."

With any freedom, the person demanding it proceeds from the necessity of the existence of a "society" and must be willing to receive this "freedom" from it. To demand that the "society" refusing the freedom in its own interest should grant it, is an absurdity as long as the "society" is more powerful than the supplicant; and to demand it when one has the power oneself, is the supreme absurdity, for then—with the power—one already has the freedom! Consequently, it can be seen that any demand for freedom from a "society" is absurd. Whoever demands a specific freedom wishes the removal of what he perceives as coercion. He does not wish the abolition of all coercion—Heaven forbid! ——He wishes of course "freedom of religion," i.e. that the practice of religion should be free. He does not wish to free himself from "religion," but he wishes to "free" "religion." Yet if we demand that everyone should enjoy "total freedom" in all things, this would presume the dissolution of all associations like state, people etc., for each one of these associations is of course obliged for reasons of self-preservation to restrict freedoms. Yet to be free of all, means to be rid of all, and so creates a phantom which is no more a man of flesh and blood than is, for example, a "citizen."

"I have no objection to freedom," says Stirner, "but I wish You more than freedom. I wish that You might not only be rid of what You do not want, but that You might also have what You do want, I wish that You might be not only a 'free man,' but 'Your own man.'—You want the freedom to enjoy delicious foods and voluptuous beds. Are men supposed to grant You this 'freedom'—are they supposed to allow You it? You do not expect that of their charity, for You know that they all think like—You Yourself. Everyone is for himself—what matters most! How, then, do You mean to arrive at the enjoyment of those foods and beds? Only by making them Your own!"

You are your own man when you make things your own; then you are more than free and more than a "higher being." Then you really *are*.

"Selfhood is My whole being and essence, is My self. I am free of what I am *rid* of; I own what I have in My power or what I *have control over*. I am *My own* at all times and under all circumstances when I know how to possess Myself and do not throw Myself away on others. I cannot really *want* being free, because I cannot make it: I can only wish for it and—strive after it, for it remains an ideal, a phantom."

"As long as even one institution continues to exist that the individual cannot dissolve, My own selfhood and ownness are far from realization.—How can I be My own when My capabilities may develop only as far as they 'do not disrupt the harmony of society'?"

The dissolution of society in every form (state, nation, people, family, humanity etc.) *is the necessary precondition for the individual, the egoist, coming into his right* and *living his own* whole real *life*. Of course, we have already seen that even in the present-day form of society the egoism of the individual is the driving force behind all actions, and we have called this individual the "reluctant egoist." Yet that is where the difference lies between him and the real, actual egoist: the former acts out of self-interest, to be sure, but with the feeling of committing an injustice to "society"; he is an egoist "who would like not to be an egoist and struggles against himself." So he is only a slave of his egoistic actions and feelings, not the master or owner of them. The first and most important condition for selfhood is that things are the property of the egoist, are *his own cause*. Here too we perceive how the word "egoism" as it is often used in a pejorative sense misses the heart of the matter:

selfishness in the usual sense of the word is not selfhood but slavery.

"Self-interest in the Christian sense," says Stirner, "means more or less this: I am 'intent only upon what benefits Me as a sensual man. Yet is sensuality My whole self? Am I wholly Myself when I am given over to sensuality? Am I following My own self, My *own* destiny, when I follow sensuality? I am *My own* only when I am in My own power and not in the power of sensuality or of any other entity (God, man, authority, law, state, Church etc.); *My self-interest* pursues what benefits Me, this master of My self or self-possessor."

Egoism, then, is not "slavery, servility, self-denial," not slavery under some master or feeling or thought—but control over them, possession of them.

"All powers dominating Me I then relegate to serving Me. Idols come into being through Me: but I need only refuse to create them anew and they no longer exist; 'higher powers' come into being only through My exalting them and degrading Myself."

My judgements and thoughts, too, can no more control me than can love or any other feeling. If I lose power to them, they control me; but if I use them as my property, which I can dispose of as I please, they are *my cause*.

"Could an egoist, then, never take sides or join a party? Yes, he could—but he cannot let the side take him or the party take him over. At all times, the party remains for him no more than a part: he is one of the party, taking part."

So then, we have moved with Stirner from destructive criticism to positive construction. We have seen how until this point the purpose of all thinking and acting was to create and maintain greater or smaller associations for the basic existence of the individual and how these "universals" pitilessly suppress anything that might endanger their welfare and permanence. We have seen, too, how egoism is the driving force behind every action of the individual and the community and how, to conceal this state of affairs, untrue and unclear concepts are alleged to control our actions. Stirner traces this entire complex mechanism back to his basic element, egoism. He does not "create" a new "fixed idea" with this, but reveals the common basis of all life's functions. And now, after the world is exposed, the egoist, the possessor of the world, stands before us in all his pristine nakedness. The thousand "concepts" and "ideas" do not exist for the true and real individual. All rigid associations are overthrown, and the millions of individuals stand face to face, each one ready to assert his will against the will of the others, to take into his possession as much of the world as he wishes—and can. What separates and unites them, the individuals, are no longer those "concepts" such as "right," "freedom," "faith," "love" etc., but *their interests*.

"What I have in My power is My own. As long as I can stand My ground as the owner, I possess the thing; if I lose it again, no matter through what power, for example through My acknowledgement of other people's right to the thing—My ownership has expired."

For millennia, men have striven to grasp the "meaning of life," to fill their lives with meaning, and have collided with the hard resistance of the world. Hundreds of systems have been devised—but the confusion has become ever greater! Millions of men have striven to emulate their "ideal models"—but no-one has succeeded! Shall this fiasco of all previous human history not have taught us that our dream "ideals" are unviable? An "ideal" devised by men was declared divine; but did that actually make it "divine"? And even if it were "divine," what then? "Divine" is not "human." In different periods, thousands have preached the "truly good," the "truly noble," the "truth," and in every head things have looked, and still look, different! Where is the critic and where is his criterion that might achieve the fulfilment of his "ideal" by some sublime medium, other than by means of force? Where is the great and powerful man who might compress all our countless desires into *one word*, *one concept*, *one ideal*, around which, as around *one* centre, things might be ordered?!

It is idle to wish for such a thing, and idle longing to wish to impress *one stamp* upon the world, to create a roof to cover everything and to devise a system into which all our wishes, thoughts and desires can be fitted! The individual alone is true and real, and he really is as he is! He might be as he ought to be if only he were not—as he is! True and real is the egoist who asserts his will to the utmost. You think that the world would fall apart if everyone were to proceed unscrupulously in the struggle of all against all? Well, then—don't we—in reality—already have the perpetual struggle of all against all?—except that freedom of movement is restricted by unnatural and untrue "concepts" and "fixed ideas."

The place of "society," the "state," the "nation" is taken over by the *association*, the union of those who have the same interests and join together in order to assert them against others. The individual belongs to this association as long as he sees his interest in it, as long as he uses it as a tool, as a means to his ends. The association is not a rigid, binding structure like "humanity," not a "higher goal" like the "nation," not a "value in itself," but a creation of the man who is his own, a tool of the egoist.

"Let Us renounce all the hypocrisy of society and recognize that if We are equal as mankind We are precisely not equal, because We are not really mankind. *Only in Our thoughts* are We equal, only when 'We' are *thought*; We are not equal as We truly are in real life. I am I, and You are I, but I am not this I that We think; and this I in which We are all equal is only *My thought*. I am a man, and You are a man, but 'man' is only an idea, only a generality; neither You nor I can be spoken. We are *unspeakable* because only *thoughts* are speakable and exist through being spoken."

It is enough for limits to be set to an individual's power through the resistance of others. If he encounters no resistance on his way, good—then he realizes that the others have no interest in hindering him or no power to do so and so have no "right." Inadequate, rigid laws are replaced by voluntary agreements on the basis of power, binding only for the person who is willing to submit to the agreement and only for as long as he does so.

"What each person needs, he should also be involved in procuring and producing; it is his own cause, his property."

"All the inhabitants of a town need bread, for example; so they could easily agree to build a public bakery."

"If men reach the point that they lose respect for property, then everyone will possess property, just as all slaves become free men as soon as they no longer respect their master as master. In this state of affairs, associations will then also multiply the individual's means and make secure the property that he has acquired through his effort."

"The individual is, however, *unique*; he is not a mere member in a party. He joins associations voluntarily and leaves them voluntarily also."

"The egoist exerts himself in a cause never for the cause's sake, but for his own sake: the cause must serve him. It is egoistic to attribute no proper or 'absolute' value to anything, but to look for its value in *Me*."

So the egoist replaces "man"! Do we have a "new man," a new "higher being," a new "fixed idea," then? Could we say that it matters nothing whether this idea is called "man" or "egoist" because as a type it is and remains a "fixed idea"?

By no means! The egoist is *not* a higher being and not a fixed idea! He is not a being at all; he is—myself—if I wish it so, and you—if you wish it. The egoist hates the words "Thou shalt" more than any others, for nothing runs more counter to his understanding of life. The preparatory work consists simply in showing what prejudices we are enmeshed in and what fixed ideas control us. And the purpose of it all is to strive to live as myself as far as I am able and, if I am interested and wish it, to convince others that, if they convert to my way of seeing things, they will better protect their own interests. The egoist is an enemy of the revolution which aims to put a "new authority" in the place of the "authority" to be overthrown. Egoism is not a "universal," is not a "concept" at all, but is a description, a definition. The new era will not be born in a day, but the teachings of egoism, if they are successful, will convince more and more individuals that their interest lies beyond the "interest of society" until such time as they are strong enough to assert their wills.—You are a believer and do not want to sacrifice your religion? We won't take it from you! See whether you can find sufficient companions to build churches together with you. Only do not demand that I and people like me should respect your teachings! If you do not disturb us, we will not concern ourselves about you. We have no interest in you. Do what you wish and can! Only what is *my cause* concerns me!

"My duty need not be to see how I realize what is *universally human*, but how I satisfy Myself. I am My own type, am without norm, without law, without model etc."

"I shall decide whether the *right* is in *Me*; *outside* of Me there is no right. If it is right with Me, it is all right. It is possible that, on that account, it is not yet right with others; that is their concern, not Mine: let them look out for themselves."

"I derive all rights and all justification from Me; I am justified in everything that I have power over. I am justified in overthrowing Zeus, Jehova, God etc. if I can; if I cannot, these gods will always be in the right against Me and in power."

"I demand no rights, and consequently need recognize none. What I can take by force, I take, and what I cannot take by force I have no right to; nor do I brag or console Myself with talk of My inalienable rights."

"There is no judge but Myself as to whether I am right or not. Others can judge and decide only whether they agree to My rights and whether they exist as rights for them too."

"What is the goal of My intercourse with the world? I want to enjoy it—which is why it must be My property and why I wish to gain it. I do not wish the freedom or the equality of man; I want only *My* power over the world, want it as My property i.e. to make it *enjoyable*."

"What, then, is *My* property? Only what is in My *power*! What property am I justified in possessing? Whatever property I *gain power over*. I give Myself the right to property by taking possession or giving Myself the *power* of possession, the authority, the permission. —Whatever people cannot wrest out of My power, remains My property."

"I, the egoist, do not have the welfare of this 'human society' at heart; I sacrifice nothing to it and only use it. In order to be able to use it fully, however, I transform it into My property and My creature, i.e. I destroy it and in its place form the *association of egoists*."

"Are those who are their own men, the egoists, a party perhaps? How could they be *their own men* if they *belonged to* a party?—Or should one side with no party? By joining others I form an *association* with them which lasts only as long as the party and I pursue one and the same goal; But though today I share the tendency of the party, even tomorrow I may no longer do so and I 'break my trust.' For Me, there is nothing *binding* (obligatory) in the party, and I do not respect it; if I no longer like it, I declare war on it."

"I already know My freedom is restricted by My inability to assert My will against another (be this other unconscious, like a rock, or conscious, like a government, an individual etc.); I deny My selfhood when—confronted by this other—I give Myself up i.e. yield, desist, surrender, show resignation, submission. For it is one thing to give up My earlier attitude because it does not lead to My goal (i.e. when I turn away from a wrong path), and it is another thing to surrender. I make a detour around a rock which is in My path until such times as I have enough powder to blow it up; I make detours around the laws of a people until I have gathered the strength to overthrow them."

"My relationship to the world, then, is this: I no longer do anything for it 'for God's sake' or 'for the sake of humanity,' but what I do I do 'for My own sake.' Only in this way does the world satisfy Me."

"For Me, no-one, not even My fellow man, is a person requiring respect, but like other beings, merely an *object*, for which I may or may not feel sympathy, an interesting or uninteresting object, a useful or useless subject.—If I can use him, I reach an understanding and join together with him in order through this agreement to strengthen *My power* and through our united force to achieve more than We could achieve alone. In this communal effort, I see absolutely no more than a multiplication of My power, and I shall continue in it only as long as it is My magnified power. In this way, however, it is—an association."

"I love people too, not only individual people, but everyone. Yet I love them with the consciousness of My egoism; I love them because love makes *Me* happy. I love because loving comes naturally to Me and I like it. I know no 'commandment of love.'"

Thus the individual is transformed into the ego, and thus Protagoras's principle is transformed when Stirner says that "not man is the measure of all things, but I am this measure."

Whether the world and other people really exist, and how they are, is interesting and significant for me—simply when it is interesting and significant for me. By accepting anything into my world, I make it my own; from the essence of things I take what has value for me to the extent that I am capable of it. I myself, however, feel myself as my ego, incomparable and unique; I know no "true ego" superior to me, no "higher man" whom I need strive to emulate, no "spiritual concepts," no "fixed ideas." *Since it is in my own interest* to live with people who think as I do, I strive to show how so far we have lived in delusion, dominated by "fixed ideas," and have renounced, our oldest and most natural right—to live for ourselves and enjoy ourselves. Our world, which is now the plaything of the most confused systems and theories and whose natural forms are concealed under a thousand veils, will not really delight us until we have made it our own and all the thousands of "spirits" have been exorcised. Then, however, each ego will be lord of the world. Ego is the creator and the creature in one, is the one and the true.

"My power is *My own*, and this is so when I know

Myself to be a *unique individual*. In the *unique individual*, even the man who is his own man returns to the creative void from which he was born. Any higher being over Me, be it God or man, weakens the feeling of My uniqueness and pales only before the sun of My self awareness. If I found My cause upon Myself, the unique individual, then it stands on the transitory, mortal creator of himself who consumes himself, and I may say: I have founded My cause on nothing."

After walking for a while with Stirner, let us now return to Protagoras and Nietzsche. Like Protagoras, Stirner knows only relative values, and for him too Protagoras's basic proposition is fundamental. Protagoras in his ethics, however, does not adopt the same ruthlessly radical and individualistic standpoint as in his theory of cognition, but introduces the "state" as a value-determining factor. Stirner, on the other hand, goes beyond this point and dissolves the "state" like any other rigid form of association, so that in his ethics, as indeed in all things, the individual alone sets and determines values. This also invalidates any "universal values" going beyond the individual and in particular any notion of "higher" or "lower" with regard to the worth of human characteristics and actions. Nietzsche too of course had attempted something similar from time to time, but in the end he could not free himself from the idea that there must be different classes of people. He calls certain individuals "higher men" and demands that his personal evaluation should be generally accepted. He is dogmatic. It is not enough for him to approach things critically; he must construct new dogmas, new ways, new hypotheses. Yet the "higher man," the "superman" and similar concepts are phantoms, "fixed ideas," like a thousand others before and since.

Basically, they are in no way different from other phantoms, such as "Christians," "socialists," "rabble," "liberals" etc., against whom Nietzsche campaigned so incisively; there is no difference between them in principle, but merely quantitatively with respect to the "human qualities" demanded of them. Just as the "Christian" and the "socialist" are to do this and that, so too must the "superman." They all belong to the same category of fantasies, and the struggle and conflict among them involves nothing real, but only "principles" and "phantoms."

That is why we consign the "superman" to the same junk heap as all the other "concepts" and "ideas." It is no more realizable than any other concept, and there will never be a "superman" any more than in two thousand years there has been one real "Christian," totally fulfilling the "Christian ideal" and a *Christian through and through*. Yet whoever finds it rewarding to pursue such an "idea" need have no fear that we will interfere, as long as he does not disturb us. The "idea chasers" should, however, finally understand that they are pursuing a "fixed idea" and that, since they lack the power, they have no right to expect others to acknowledge their "fixed idea." It is ludicrous and tasteless to complain about other people's inability to appreciate our own "ideas."

It seems to me the most monstrous fact in world history that men have constantly and persistently clung to "fixed ideas," and that such idols and "saints" have continued to exist even in ages when the gods themselves—likewise only created by man in his own image—were buried.

This striving to attribute "higher value" to things, to dress them up and demand that other people should acknowledge these "values," reminds one of the games played by children. The childish imagination breathes life into inanimate pieces of wood and cardboard, so creating an entire world—in whose actual reality, however, the children require observers to believe.

Anyone looking at things even once without prejudice, totally without prejudice, must realize that their alleged value and significance is nothing more than what we ourselves attribute to them and that, when we no longer acknowledge their significance, their significance no longer exists.

I, however, ask the person who talks of the value of things: *How do you wish to make me understand the value that you attach to a thing*? How can you make me feel what you wish to express? You have no means of testing what impression your judgement or opinion evokes in me! You say that to be brave is good. Supposing even that you could state precisely and exactly what "good" is! How can you make me understand *what your "good" is*, since at any time you can speak to me only in relative terms, which we no more have in common than what you want to explain to me.

So I am not only to accept your concept "good," but I am to do so without even knowing what you mean by it in your heart!

If you can understand this, you can finally understand that every individual is isolated and that the impossibility of testing and checking our means of communication necessarily makes us "unique."

To believe in "ideas" means in reality *believing in the "idea" that I construct of your "idea"*! A phantom, doubly a phantom, a labyrinth of nonsense and delusion.

The impossibility of communicating on another person's understanding of his own values—which seems to me the most stable and natural foundation for egoism—has never yet been examined, not even by Stirner. The question lies outside the scope of this work, but is a new and important factor for the philosophy of egoism and will be the subject of a future investigation.

Appendix.

Index to Benedict Lachmann's
Der Individualistische Anarchist

Biographical Sketch:

As a young man frequenting bohemian circles, Benedict Lachmann met John Henry Mackay (1864 – 1933). Mackay introduced Lachmann to the egoism of Max Stirner.

Lachmann wrote *Protagoras, Nietzsche, Stirner / ein Beitrag zur Philosophie des Individualismus und Egoismus* (Protagoras – Nietzsche – Stirner / A Contribution to the Philosophy of Individualism and Egoism) in 1914. A 1978 edition of this book was published by Kurt Zube's Mackay-Gesellschaft (Mackay Society). Kurt is the father of John Zube, the creator of the Peace Plans / Libertarian Microfiche Project.

Lachmann opened a bookstore in 1919, the same year of publication as his magazine *Der individualistische Anarchist*. In the 1930s he turned over his bookshop to an assistant. As a Jewish man and an individualist he was unable to operate a bookshop in National Socialist Germany. Lachmann was in the first group of Jews deported from Berlin. He died in Ghetto Litzmannstadt in the city of Łódź, Poland, on December 4th, 1941.

—Trevor Blake

Prospectus:

Der individualistische anarchist asks those in whose hands this booklet comes who are ignorant of the principles of individualistic anarchism to pay attention to the explanations below. Anarchism is against authority, its goal is order and freedom. Unfortunately, it is still not superfluous to repeat that anarchism and anarchy are not disorder and are not chaos. Only the antiquated idea that order without domination is not possible has created and sustains this misuse of the word anarchism.
[...] Freedom is both an aim and a means for the anarchist. He therefore rejects every violent conversion, every compulsion, and, like every dictatorship, abhors every dictatorial means. He wishes to remain unpolluted in his affairs as long as he is not aggressive, and not to harass others unless they become aggressive with him. Individualistic Anarchism is not a party; it is a free association of those who seek their personal freedom. Anyone who wants to belong to this association, as long as he wants it.

—Benedict Lachmann
(April 1st, 1919).

Index of Issues:

No. 1 | April 1st, 1919

Der individualistische Anarchist (Vorwort) by Benedict Lachmann	1
Fruhlingslied by Georg Herwegh	4
Der Anarchist von heute by Arthur Kahane	5
Und das Licht? by Benedict Lachmann	10
Der Wanderer by Friedrich Dobe	20
Ein unbekannter Stirner-Brief (Facsimile) by Benedict Lachmann	40
Die Frau und der Freie by Johanna Salzmann	42

No. 2 | April 16th, 1919

Der individualistische Anarchist by Benedict Lachmann	53
Staat und Ordnung by Antibarbarus	56
Die Pflicht des burgerlichen Ungehorsams by Friedrich Dobe	61
Sozialisierung oder genossenschaftliche Betriebweise? by Hugo Nansen	83
Polen, Preussen und Deutschland by Benedict Lachmann	88
Jugendbewegung by Fritz Gross	94

No. 3 | May 1st, 1919

Der individualistche Anarchist (Vorwort)
by Benedict Lachmann — 97

Die konstitutionelle genossenschaftliche Fabrik
by Hugo Nansen — 100

Drei Traume in der Wuste unter einem Mimosenbaum
by Margarethe Dobe — 114

Die Kosten des burgerlichen Ungehorsams
by Friedrich Dobe — 122

Der Einzelne und die Gesellschalt
by Antibarbarus — 126

Zwischen Tod und Tod
by Johanna Salzmann — 131

Die Ubergangssozialisten
by Benedict Lachmann — 135

No. 4 | May 15th, 1919

Der individualistische Anarchist (Vorwort)
by Benedict Lachmann — 145

Das Gelt
by Friedrich Dobe — 148

Gesetz und Autoritat
by Kropotkin — 157

Zur Zeit
by Friedrich Partmuss — 180

Der "sozialistische" Tolstoj
by Gerhard Lehmann — 183

Aus den Papieren eines gefallen Soldaten
by Karl Ludwig — 188

No. 5 | June 1st, 1919

Der individualistische Anarchist (Vorwort)
by Benedict Lachmann — 195

Das Monopol als Quelle des sozialen Ubels
by Hugo Nansen — 198

Die Provinzial-Landbank
by Friedrich Dobe — 212

Verstaatlichung des Menschen oder Vermenschlichung des Staates
by Heinz Blucher — 220

Der Einzelne und die Politik
by Antibarbarus — 225

Kultur des Individualismus
by Walter Goldschmidt — 232

Einst
by Ludmillavon Rehren — 241

No. 6 | June 15th, 1919

Der individualistische Anarchist (Vorwort)
by Benedict Lachmann — 247

Bolschewismus und Anarchismus
by Benedict Lachmann — 250

Das Erbrecht und der Staat
by Hugo Nansen — 261

Die Verwicklichung der Freiheit
by Friedrich Dobe — 272

Herr Rathenau im Neuen Staate
by Gerhard Lehmann — 280

Wie wird die Schuld gesuhnt
by Maximilian Raven — 282

No. 7 | July 1st, 1919

Die Waffen es Einzelnen wider den Staat 289
by Friedrich Dobe

Kunstliche Monopole (Kartellierung und Vertrustung der industriellen Produktion) 311
by Hugo Nansen

Die Logik der Gesetze by 311
Benedict Lachmann

Von der Grundlage aller Sittlichkeit 315
by Kropotkin

Briefwechsel mit Herrn Johan Pedersen in Aarhus 320
by Benedict Lachmann

No. 8 | July 15th, 1919

Aufruf 337
by Benedict Lachmann

Pierre Joseph Proudhon (mit einem Portrat) 338
by Friedrich Dobe

Kunstliche Monopole (Kartellierung und Vertrustung der industriellen Produktion) II 347
by Hugo Nansen

Von der Freiheit und ob es sie gibt 361
by Antibarbarus

Dichter sterben 367
by Friedrich Partmuss

Richard Beer-Hofmann; Jaakobs Traum 369
by Eduard Saenger

No. 9 | August 1st, 1919

Aufruf   373
by Benedict Lachmann

Kreig und Vernunft   374
by Leo Tolstoy

Kunstliche Monopole (Kartellierung und Vertrustung der industriellen Produktion) III   381
by Hugo Nansen

Das geistige Eigentum under der Anarchismus   396
by Benedict Lachmann

No. 10 | August 15th, 1919

Aufruf   409
by Benedict Lachmann

Panarchie   410
by M.N.

Verpflichtung   417
by Eugen Styx

Kautsky's Richtlinien fur ein sozialistisches Aktionsprogram   423
by Hugo Nansen

Zwei Bucher aus Stirners Besitz   436
by Friedrich Dobe

Bucherbesprechungen und Anzeigen   439

No. 11 | September 1st, 1919

Aufruf b
y Benedict Lachmann — 445

Freie Sozialisierung
by MaxG. Grossmann — 446

Ein Politiker vor dem Zeil, von Auberon Herbert, aus dem Enlischen
by Friedrich Dobe — 461

Diskussion (Das geistige Eigentum und der Anarchismus) — 476

Notizen
by Issue 11 — 484

No. 12 | September 15th, 1919

Der individualistische Anarchist
by Benedict Lachmann — 485

Ein Politiker vor dem Zeil (II)
by Friedrich Dobe — 487

Vom Segen des Zwanges
by Antibarbarus — 507

Diskussion (Die konstitutionelle, genossenschaftliche Fabrik) — 507

Pierre Ramus gegen Marx
by Kurt Sonnefeld — 515

www.ingramcontent.com/pod-product-compliance
Lightning Source LLC
Chambersburg PA
CBHW030857040426
R18081800001B/R180818PG42333CBX00001B/1